BECOMING FREE

AYANNA N. PARRENT

Silvi ~
I am so glad to be
in your world now

Ayanna

Cover Design: Wicked Whale Publishing
Interior Design: Wicked Whale Publishing
Editor: Kat Szmit
Photos: Kristie Gillooly Dean, Lydia Leclair Photography, and Ayanna N. Parrent

Parrent, Ayanna N. pp 210

Becoming Free/ Ayanna N. Parrent

Summary: One woman's story of addiction, recovery, and forgiveness through the healing power love, yoga, and motherhood.

ISBN: 9798588092418

Printed in the United States of America

To those who have passed on . . .

Valerie Gail Lake, Fern Cunningham-Terry , & Joseph Dimaggio - To my mom for showing me what a badass woman is, especially rocking an afro. To Fern for being all of our mothers and creating shapes that changed our lives. To Joe for seeing me when I couldn't see myself . To the black and brown families who have lost loved ones due to racism and police brutality, I love you. To the the families who have lost loved ones to addiction, I love you.

To those keeping me going . . .

Blessing Lake Parrent, Jason Parrent, Emily Bibbins Silas, Ian Downing Kilpatrick, & Thea James. Sean and Holden for giving me the privilege of being their mom. Blessing for being my never ending teacher and embodying the best of me and my mom combined. Jason for being my constant steady and allowing me to be myself. Emily for being my best friend, always. Ian for being my brother and teaching me love beyond myself. Thea for bringing light into places when I think I can only see dark.

FIND · RECOVER · EVOLVE · ENJOY

F.R.E.E.

B

CONTENTS

PROLOGUE

It was a Friday near the end of June, the sun casting rays of warmth, possibility and hope upon the little Cape Cod town where I lived. I remember that much. But neither the sparklingly clear blue skies, nor the brilliant sunshine could erase the fact that I felt, to my core, like complete shit. Worse, in fact.

My day had begun much the same as many of the days before it, with some kind of drink, probably wine since that was my poison of choice back then. I couldn't function without it, or so I believed. I believed so many lies back then; too many to count.

Somehow, I managed to get the daughter my husband and I were in the process of adopting off to preschool, keeping up the appearance of the devoted, dedicated mother. But appearances can be deceiving, as I knew well. Thankfully, or not, no one seemed to notice that I'd already been drinking in spite of the early hour.

With Blessing safe at school, I tried doing "normal" things, tidying the house, making sure we had food in the fridge, but as the morning's alcohol wore off, I needed a refill and took myself out for a liquid lunch of lots of chardonnay and little, if any, food. Before long, the tensions eased and I began to feel better, the wine dulling my emotions.

But it couldn't dull the fact that it was nearing time to pick Blessing up from preschool. Through glossy eyes, I peered at myself in the restroom mirror, my face puffy from drink, eyes struggling to focus. Self-loathing roared to the forefront of everything else. All I could feel was a deep and murky hatred of myself and what I'd become. I had become the one person I'd sworn I'd never emulate, and my life was crumbling around me because of it.

I had become my mother.

❧ I ❧

WAITING

It was cold, the kind that seeps into your skin past your clothes, making you feel as though you will never be warm again. But I stood, outside, resolutely, counting the train cars of the Newton area transportation system as they passed by. Each time another pulled into the station, I'd unknowingly hold my breath, watching each passenger disembark, scanning the crowd for my mother's hair, my mother's face.

They said she was coming. The guys on the phone told me she would show up for real this time, promised me she'd be there. Shivering, I stared down the tracks, miles upon miles of steel and wood, hoping the next one would be the one carrying her.

I began to count the trains. I counted 43. Forty-three trains went by, all green, each one full as it pulled into the station, emptying itself of another wave of passengers before pulling out again.

This can't be right, I thought. Not again.

My throat began to close as I fought back the tears burning

my eyes, battling back the realization that I'd been had again. I'd been suckered into thinking that seeing her again was possible. Though only 9, I'd walked the four miles from my father's house to the train station because the men on the phone had assured me my mother would be there.

My mother had cautioned me many times not to be gullible, that women were always smarter than men, and to be careful who you trusted. I trusted her, and for some reason couldn't let that go. I held onto that notion as tightly as a child holds a blanket, as if the material, the threads, were a part of the tapestry of their soul.

Suddenly, a voice interrupted my thoughts.

"You okay?" Asked the man that worked in the train station, who had been watching me outside through a window. Inside, where he was, it was warm and cozy. I couldn't feel my toes.

"Yes," I said with a falsely bubbly smile, belying the turmoil within. "My friend is just late."

"Okay," he said. "Suit yourself. But come inside if you want."

I could tell it was warm inside. There was a small café, and likely plenty of chairs in which I could sit and wait where it was warm. I gazed up at the brick station house and never felt more alone. Didn't he know I couldn't go inside? That I didn't deserve to be in there, comfortable, cozy, and safe? What if I missed her and she didn't see me and decided to leave? It would be my fault, again.

Another train was coming. This had to be it. I exhaled, not realizing I'd been once again holding my breath. The excitement of her potential arrival built in the same way it does on the first big hill of a roller coaster, butterflies in my stomach and my heart racing. The corners of my mouth began to curl up. I just knew she would be on this train. She had to be.

❧ 2 ❧

MS. VALERIE LAKE

Her name was Valerie Gail Lake and she was a badass. Fiercely independent, she rocked a huge afro, which complemented her smooth, coffee-colored skin, dotted with a constellation of tiny brown moles characteristic of every woman in her family. She was incredibly smart, a true force of nature. She was also an addict and an alcoholic, illnesses that made her completely unreliable, as well as unpredictable. I just knew her as Mom, someone I loved ferociously, and also hated with a similar passion at times.

When I was born, I knew nothing of my mother's challenged past, which also included an alcoholic mother who took to locking Valerie in closets so she wouldn't have to deal with her. I just knew that sometimes my mother was around, but mostly she wasn't.

The night my mother went into labor with me, she told no one. Why? Chinese food had just been ordered from her favorite restaurant and she wasn't missing that for anything, not even my birth. She knew that if she told anyone she was in labor, they wouldn't let her have her Chinese food, as you're not supposed to have a big meal before delivery.

When she'd finished her dinner, the food happily filling her belly, she announced, "Well, time to go to the hospital!" Wide eyes stared back at her in amazement, no one making the connection. Neither did anyone make a move to help her. "I've been in labor for about an hour now, but damned if I wasn't going to get that Chinese food," she told them with a smirk.

Soon, she was bound for the hospital where I was born from her will, tenacity, and a belly full of Chinese food. Funny thing about it being Chinese food: I was born to a black mother and a white father and came out looking incredibly Asian. Apparently, my great grandfather had some Asian in him and it clearly transferred to my genes.

My mother wasn't super surprised, but some of the hospital staff were. After a bath, they brought the tiny bundle back to my mother, who took one look at the swaddled infant and screamed. "That's not my baby!" Everyone looked confused as they gazed at the beautiful baby with the round head, big, wide eyes, a few soft curls of hair, and coffee-colored skin. "*My* baby looks Asian!" My mother told the nurse, rolling her eyes in exasperation. "You idiots! That's *not* my kid!"

The nurse looked closely at the identification tag connecting mother to child, her cheeks flaming crimson when she realized her error. Slowly, she wheeled that beautiful biracial baby back to the nursery and brought my mother her actual child, me, the one with the pear-shaped head that inspired my nickname, Yani Pear. Did I mention that my mother was obsessed with pears?

In the beginning, we were a family of three – my mother, my father, and me. My parents met in New York during the heady days of Martin Luther King, Jr., and Malcolm X. My parents were full-on Malcom X supporters, with my father something of a leader of the anti-racist movement at Northeastern University in spite of his being white.

Articles were written about him and how he worked to teach white people how not to be racist. When he embarked on some genealogy and discovered that a great grandfather was Cape Verdean, he suddenly identified as a person of color, seeming to forget that he was mainly white.

We lived at a place called The Gifford School, a therapeutic school for special needs children struggling with mental and behavioral issues. A woman named Margaret Gifford started the school in 1964 in Weston, Massachusetts. My mom and Margaret were very close, to the point that when Gifford was just getting started and needed caretakers, my mother and father signed on, moving from New York to Weston. My father took care of the grounds and taught gym classes and my mom helped Margaret with whatever she needed.

I was born nearby and lived with my parents at the school until I was six years old, in a small apartment on the top floor of an older building that had a kitchen, living room, and two bedrooms. This is the place where my parents' marriage disintegrated, and where I heard them fight through the thin walls of the cramped space. This was where I became old at a very young age.

Though initially smitten with my father, in time my mother came to loathe him. She was constantly appalled by his behavior and intensely frustrated by his victim mindset, which took on new depth after learning his ancestry. My father used his lineage as an excuse to avoid so many responsibilities, including parenting me.

When they separated around the time I was six, I was elated. I remember waking up one night to find blood everywhere in our humble home. My parents had had a huge fight, both drinking, and somehow my mother had hit her face on the television, her mouth bleeding profusely. It looked like a war zone. They downplayed the situation, but I knew that my dad had a temper, and while I still don't know exactly what took place, I had my guesses.

I took solace in the Gifford School, loved by the students and Margaret. My mother had taught me early to love kids, especially those who struggle, something I learned about firsthand at Gifford. Each student had some kind of behavioral problem, and each also had a story. A reason to be there. I came to see their challenges as superpowers rather than deficits. Regardless of their issues, they were always kind to me and as a result, the school was my playground.

One of my favorite Gifford School stories happened after a significant snowstorm. It was up to my mother and Margaret to call the staff and let them know whether there was school. On this day, even though every other district around had canceled classes, my mother and Margaret told the Gifford staff that yes, there was still school.

They rolled in frustrated and angry that they had to work. But there was something in the air. As they pulled up the driveway, the tantalizing scent of bacon and eggs permeated the breeze. My mom and Margaret had planned a brunch surprise for everyone, right down to the Bloody Marys and champagne, much to the delight and bewilderment of each staff member.

The snow day brunch became something of a tradition, taking place at least once a winter, the returning staff never letting the new members in on the event in order to ensure their surprise. It also became a story I loved hearing, and one my mother loved to tell, which was good since I begged her to tell it as many times as she could. I enjoyed watching the expression on her face as she got more and more excited, describing how stunned each staff member was. I realized it was more than staff. It was family.

In spite of struggling with formal education, my mother was a voracious reader who, during her high school years, read every single book in the school library and taught herself the materials within. Eventually, she got a job with WGBH, Boston's Channel 2. She was on the front lines, doing impressive administrative work. From my regular visits to the station, I knew that my mother was well liked and well respected by her colleagues. If they knew about her drinking problem, they never said a word.

I don't think there were many moments when my mother was sober, her days and nights fueled by alcohol, cocaine, and god knows what else. I remember visiting a coffee shop with her as a child and commenting on the rich scent of the coffee, confused as to why she was unable to smell it, wondering whether she had a cold. I had no clue that all the coke had destroyed not only her sense of smell, but the inside of her nose, as well.

It was shortly after the bloody fight that my parents called it quits. But what I didn't know until much later was that my father had started a relationship with an English teacher at the Gifford school, a woman named Maggie, whom he later married.

I don't have all the information about what happened back then, but I know that given my father's track record, there was surely some crossover regarding both relationships, though I can't imagine my mother with her addictions was very present for any relationship at the time.

After my dad left, eventually marrying Maggie, my mother and I bounced around, staying at different friends' houses before getting an apartment in Cambridge. I divided my time between that apartment and my father's house in Newton and the contrast between the two couldn't have been sharper. In Cambridge no one noticed the color of my mixed-race skin, and if they did, no one cared.

But in Newton, a predominantly white part of Massachusetts, I stood out like a beacon on a dark night. Fortunately, I only had to go there part time, far more comfortable with my Cambridge life than that in Newton for myriad reasons.

Somewhere around the age of 10, still splitting my time between Cambridge and Newton, I found my mother dangerously drunk in our home. Nearly every surface of our tiny apartment was covered with liquor bottles of all colors, shapes, and sizes. They were everywhere.

My mother had invited some guy over, and right in front of me, they began having sex as if I wasn't there. Soon, they were both buck naked, having sex on the porch of the apartment. I was so angry, I took all of the bottles that still had something in them and dumped them down the drain. I, in my childlike logic, decided that I was going to take away their "juice."

My saving grace was the after-school program I attended at a magnet school in Cambridge, with one of my favorite teachers, a woman who had the kids sing Beatles songs and do projects on fighting the power. She'd break down the Beatles' lyrics and we'd hold little concerts, do gymnastics, and delight in creative endeavors. She was progressive as hell and wonderful. I adored her. She was integral in keeping what little self-esteem I had from turning to dust.

I told someone in the program about my mother and her drinking and neglect, but nothing happened. No one came to save me. Instead, I was often the last kid to leave at night. On so many nights, my mother just didn't come. I'd be sitting there for hours, waiting, fear gnawing a hole in my little belly.

Since my mother didn't have a license and therefore didn't drive, when she'd finally show up, she was usually stumbling out of a cab, somehow armed with the cash necessary to pay the late fees incurred by my overtime. Her excuses were constant. I'm still confused as to why no one called my father. If they did, why didn't he come? My only guess is that such calls back then were governed by the rules of shared custody, and since it was my mother's time with me, my dad simply wasn't contacted when the program hours ended and my mother wasn't there.

When I was home, I was often alone, left with no food, no money, and no idea when my mother would return. Sometimes, hungry and fearful, I'd cave and end up calling my father and Maggie, retreating to the illusion of safety that was their home in Newton. While not alcohol-fueled and violent like my mom's place in Cambridge, it wasn't nurturing, though it was safe enough for a scared kid to regroup at.

Other times I'd venture to a local playground to bide my time while I waited for her to come home. When she didn't, I'd just call my dad. Again. More often than I'd prefer to recall, I'd go home and find her passed out cold, forced to call my father in order to eat or be in a relatively safe space for the night.

THEN MY MOTHER LOST THE APARTMENT IN CAMBRIDGE, relegating me to my father's house full time as she became homeless, sleeping between train tracks, in cars, or in a homeless shelter in Central Square. Reconciling the contrast between her obvious intellect and the fact that she was a homeless addict was immensely difficult.

Eventually, she secured a spot in a homeless shelter for women and children, but in order to stay there she had to be sober. She also had to have me with her. She'd been in other shelters but had likely been kicked out due to her drinking. She soon got word that she'd have to leave this shelter, at Government Center, but not because of her drinking. Instead, she had to leave since she didn't technically have a child with her full time.

I only stayed with her during my allotted time with her, crying because of the stark circumstances the people there were living in, including tiny babies. Even as a kid I knew that home-less shelters in Boston were no place for a baby, let alone a middle schooler.

Despite how horrible the shelter was, my mother tried her damnedest to get me to stay with her so that she could keep her room there, but I knew I had to leave. I remember calling my father in Newton, where I had my own bed in my own room and told him I couldn't go back there to that frightening, degrading place. Not for the first time, my mother told me she hated me and that I'd ruined her life. Getting kicked out of the shelter was my fault.

"If you really loved me, you'd stay with me at the shelter," she said, calling forth the manipulation tactic I'd heard countless times before.

The guilt was massive. I genuinely felt I'd ruined her life, and saw it as my job to fix it, even though, as a pre-teen, I lacked any of the tools to do so. But I also knew that I had to go, had to leave her in the shelter and try to find some semblance of safety at my dad's.

It would be nearly a decade before I saw my mother again, but I certainly tried. I can't tell you how many times I stood at the train station watching for her, waiting, only to be let down time and again.

3

IN ABSENTIA

I want to say that I wasn't used to being disappointed by my mother, but I can't. For us, it seemed like just a way of being, but since I had nothing to compare it to, I wasn't aware of how dysfunctional my family truly was.

My mom wasn't at my high school graduation. She wasn't there for a lot of my milestones – lost teeth, a top test grade, birthdays. I remember getting my period and my mother not being there to help me understand what was happening and what to do. Instead, I had to turn to my stepmother, who rose to the occasion as best she could, but we both knew it wasn't the same.

Maggie wasn't perfect, but she tried. While I don't recall not liking her or our relationship being extremely difficult, she seems to. One day I was goofing off in the backyard, acting silly and walking in a way I considered funny in my youthfulness. Suddenly, Maggie came outside, visibly upset. For years, she'd lived with back problems and pain, and mistook my youthful exuberance as nastiness. She told me that I didn't need to make fun of her by pretending to walk funny. I was legit confused. I had no idea what she was so angry about.

That was my first introduction to her sensitive nature, something that would color our relationship from that point onward, continuing to this day. I was just a goofy kid trying to entertain myself while all alone in my dad's yard, something she took personally. Mimicking her or mocking her wasn't my thing, and definitely wasn't how I would have entertained myself, ever.

Her own life had been difficult, something I won't ever discount. Both of her parents had died of alcoholism and it affected her greatly. Trauma, as I'd learn, has a way of clouding the lenses through which we see the world, shaping us as children in ways that are difficult to alter in adulthood.

As my relationship with my mother worsened due to her addictions, Maggie did her best to be there. She came to school meetings, showed up at camp on visiting day, and for these moments I was grateful. But her generosity was conditional and based on whether I felt a certain way or responded in accordance to what she had given me. It was a shadow over our relationship that only grew as we both got older. It seems I was destined not to be properly mothered.

Strangely, though my own mother hurt me in myriad ways multiple times, I idolized her. She was so powerful in what she said and in how she loved me, in spite of her behavior. Even when she looked like a hot mess, I was aware of the powerful woman within. I'd seen it the few times she'd gotten sober and clear-headed. She'd make sure we had time together and was keen on sharing her wisdom, which often involved drawing on her feminism. In spite of her illnesses, she instilled in me strong values that remain with me to this day.

To say that my mother had a dark past would be an understatement. It was so strained, so painful that I wasn't allowed to meet her mother, my grandmother, until I was 18 years old. She was that abusive. To help explain it to me, my mom would have me watch "Mommie Dearest," a horribly traumatizing film. Apparently, my mother's mother was very much like the central character, a terrifyingly abusive, narcissistic woman who once beat her daughter with wire clothes hangers.

My mother seemed to gravitate toward similar abuse. When I was somewhere between the ages of 8 and 10, my mother dated a horribly abusive man who knocked her front teeth out. I'd been at my father's and the next time I saw my mother her teeth were gone. When I asked why, she not only didn't evade the question, she told me what had happened despite my not being old enough for such heavy information.

But I often got different versions of her stories. When she was sober, she'd minimize the more frightening details. But when she was drunk, they'd come rolling out, leaving me shocked and stunned, trying to come to terms with such a powerful woman being left toothless by someone she let into her life. It didn't make sense then, and in many ways, still doesn't.

Relationships were not her forte. While working at WGBH, my mother had an affair with a married man. They seemed madly in love, but she was drinking, which certainly tinged their connection with a negative light. Another time, I remember walking on a beach with my mother and some other man, who started beating her openly. To this day I continue to wonder why I was allowed to remain in such instability.

I have faint memories of people in Cambridge keeping an eye on me, though no one said anything about the conditions I was living in. Even some validation about their awareness of the situation would have been helpful, but there was none. I remember telling so many adults about my mother, about her drinking and her not waking up, and nothing happened.

Nothing was done. I told the mother of one of my two childhood friends about her, hoping in my youthful innocence that she might offer some answers, insight into what was wrong with her, with me.

I ached with a loneliness no child should ever feel, knowing that I was different, that my life, my family, everything was different from other people. I couldn't name what that difference was, though. I just knew my mother had some problems. I knew she'd get sloppy, the house in disarray, and that she often wouldn't sleep at night. I even knew it had to do with alcohol, but I didn't yet have the awareness to put the myriad pieces together.

I think part of the issue with people's reluctance to help was my parents' interracial marriage, which even then, more than a decade after the Civil Rights Movement, and in a bustling city, albeit one in New England, was still considered taboo. It probably didn't help that my mother was volatile, and my father detached and more interested in his own ego.

If any child tells a story like mine these days, of a mother passed out cold, bottles of liquor strewn about, Child Services would be at the door in a heartbeat. But back then, it seemed that people were more comfortable averting their eyes and avoiding my truth.

School should have been a godsend, and in many ways, it was, but I struggled with the academic aspects. I was an average student that didn't put much effort in. The truth was that my brain was so muddled with worry that I couldn't retain the information. Throughout each school day, my mind was on overdrive, worrying about my mother. Is she okay? Will she come get me today? What is she like today? Is she breathing? Is she alive?

This kind of thinking, this pervasive worry, seemed normal to me then. It's only now, as the mother of my own daughter, that

I'm beginning to see just how fucked up it really was, and what a detrimental effect it had on my learning.

It didn't help that there seemed to be some sort of odd connection between my mother and the principal of my school. I recall them talking often, and him treating me especially nice, always checking up on me. When I reflect back now, I see that people were often overly nice, as if they knew. But if that's true, then why didn't anyone intervene?

A part of what kept me going was the surreal nature of so many things that were happening. It was as if my mind would brush up against the trauma, refusing to grasp it because of the immensity of it all. So, I'd separate. I'd stuff my emotions deep within, refusing to acknowledge them.

How my poor academic progress was continuously overlooked by so many educators is beyond me. Between the constant worry and teachers overlooking my issues, there were huge gaps in what I'd learned compared to other students. That further fed my already low self-esteem since not being able to retain what seemed like basic information made me feel incredibly stupid. I felt awful about myself all the time. Never mind that I was already dealing with complicated messages from my mother through her chaotic actions that she didn't really love me. Now I couldn't measure up in school. I kept trying to do the work but couldn't.

I thought something must have been wrong with me, that I was broken in some way. Sadly, no one was telling me otherwise, and if they were, I certainly didn't hear them above everything that was constantly crashing around me. And yet, teachers kept moving me along, right up to high school where suddenly my educational deficits were many, and finally noticed.

But before that came many years of doing little else other than just surviving.

❧ 4 ❧

STILL WAITING

I pictured my mother reading a new book on the train, wondering if maybe she'd become so engrossed in the story that she'd missed her stop, the one where I was waiting in the biting cold. I could see it in my young mind, her eyes so glued to the pages that she forgot to look up at her surroundings as they sped past in a blur from cityscape to tree-lined suburb.

She always had to be the first to read new works by African American authors. She craved all the stories of those that came before her the way a broken heart longs for its lost love. I honestly had no idea whether, at this point in her life and in her illness, she was still reading regularly. I just hoped it was the reason for her delay. I honestly had no idea whether she was even alive. I prayed she was.

I closed my eyes, squeezing them tight, clenching my fingers into fists as I prayed to a god that, according to my mother, didn't exist. If it did, she'd told me, life wouldn't be so horrible. "All those stupid folks praying to nothing in AA," she would say. "Don't they know if god was real, no one would need AA? Girls wouldn't get raped or locked in closets, and black folks wouldn't get so hurt."

God or not, real or false, I still prayed that day as the cold wormed its way through my clothes and into my very marrow. I couldn't bear to open my eyes and not see her. Again. I pleaded with god that I just wanted to say hi this time. I promised.

Another train pulled in, exchanged its passenger load, and pulled away. It was getting dark. Time to call it.

I walked, my head down, hunched against the cold that wasn't just from the New England chill, listening to my footsteps throughout each of the four miles it took to get home. I was numb with cold and hollow with disappointment.

When I got home, the phone rang, a wall-mounted, sunshine yellow thing with a rotary dial and a long, curly cord like a strange tail. The ring was annoying and sounded like the screech of the braking trains on the steel rails back at the station.

I hesitated for a brief moment as I always did, then answered, as I always did.

"Hello?" The background noise sounded like a party in full swing. I heard lots of men laughing, singing, and coughing.

"Oh, hey sweetheart!" A man's voice said. "She really wanted to come, but she got sick this time. But she really wanted to see you!"

I could hear the tinny laughter of women in the background now and my mind wasn't sure whether to label her as one of the ones laughing. I said nothing and hung up the phone with the cackles and coughs echoing forth as I set the receiver into its cradle.

Suddenly, the front door burst open. "How was Caity's?" My stepmother asked.

"Great," I mumbled. Not even my best friend Caity knew this had been the fifth time I had walked alone to the train station, where I'd waited all day for my mother to arrive as promised. This *had* to be the last time. Suck it up, Buttercup. *Who cares?* I told myself. I resolved not to do it again, no matter who called, no matter how much my mother begged me. I was done.

But... She still loved me, right? Of course she still loved me. Right? As my adolescent mind went to war with contrasting messages - her voice saying yes, while her actions clearly indicated no - I realized then that the truth was that it really didn't matter anymore. For me, the innocence of life was gone, probably for good, buried with the vulnerability that I would not allow to see the light of day again.

That night, I made sure that my secret bag of makeup, especially my favorite bright pink lipstick, was carefully tucked into my backpack, ready for school the next day. This time I swore that I'd be brave. This time I swore that I'd be strong as I put on that new face, that careful mask, that I wouldn't let it slip again.

5

BLOOD ON SNOW

When my mother lost the apartment, our place to live, I went from dividing my time between my parents to living with my father and his wife full time. Where Cambridge, even in all of its New England whiteness, was still relatively diverse to the point where a biracial kid was not much of a thing, Newton was the polar opposite.

In Cambridge, my mom and I blended almost seamlessly into the tapestry of the city. I say "almost" because her drinking resulted in some seriously dropped stitches. We could walk down the sidewalks unnoticed, unless my mother was stumbling in her uncoordinated drunkenness.

In Newton I stuck out like blood on snow. Not only was I not white, as seemingly 99 percent of the population was at the time (though I doubt much has changed), but I was also not a slender girl. What made it worse, as superficial as this sounds, is that I didn't own a single pair of Guess jeans, which was the unofficial uniform of every teenage girl in sight.

The bullying was so intense that when I saw a pair of Guess

jeans at a local yard sale, I begged Maggie to buy them for me. I wore them proudly that Monday, finally feeling like I'd fit in. I couldn't have been more wrong. The moment my classmates saw them, they tore into me, telling me how outdated they were, among other less friendly comments, including one from a girl claiming the jeans used to be hers. I realized, sadly, that she was probably right.

Compounding my challenges, it became clear that there were some major holes in my learning. It was finally noticed that I'd been shunted along regardless of lacking even basic skills in certain areas, particularly math. Math was at the top of the list of subjects that were the bane of my existence. I hadn't learned a thing.

Math is a subject akin to building something. In the elementary grades, ideally, you learn the basics – addition, subtraction, division, multiplication – and create a sturdy foundation on which to build upon with aspects like fractions, geometry, calculus, and even physics. My foundation was cracked and missing parts, which meant building anything on top of it was fruitless. Thank god for calculators.

Because of the obvious gaps in my learning, there were numerous meetings about me in high school. Concerns were raised more than once about how I'd been passed along, teachers in my former school in Cambridge seeming to take no notice of how many deficits I had. But in spite of the meetings and the impassioned discussions, not much was done to genuinely help me.

But there was one area in which I shined. Somewhere along the way, between those first tentative days of kindergarten and the more aware moments of the pre-teen years I'd discovered writing. Writing, keeping a journal, was the one place where I could be fully me, uninterrupted, undampened. I was free to pour my thoughts onto the pages, and I did, often and with gusto. My passions, my innermost thoughts, and my dreams all spilled out in various colors of ink.

Writing gave me the gift of connecting with my emotions, as painful as they were. Each page was a safe space for me to express what had been bottled up, and each word written fueled my appreciation for English class. By the time I became a junior in high school, I was in Advanced English, which seems unthinkable given the aforementioned learning deficits.

But it was kind of cool to have that experience of finally being good at something. There was so little I felt truly good at, so I relished the feeling and looked forward to almost every English class I had.

In high school, where every other kid was partying it up on the weekends in some family mansion, I was adamantly against drinking and shunned that lifestyle, mainly because I now understood that my mother was an alcoholic. In the background of that awareness was the realization that all of the chaos in my life with her, the instability, the being left at after school, the uncertainty, the confusion, all of the violence and neglect, was also attributable to her drinking, but I wasn't prepared to go there. I had enough on my emotional plate with just trying to make it through high school.

Miraculously, and not with the best GPA, I did. Somehow, astonishingly, I was accepted into a nearby college, mainly on the strength of a well-written essay. I enrolled at Wheelock College near Fenway Park in Boston and soon began hanging out with college dudes. It was actually a wonderful time. I became passionate about race issues and my writing took off, with one of my essays published in the school library.

I felt as if I mattered, perhaps for the first time. I felt like I was making a huge difference in the world and was living my life as normally as possible. I no longer find it ironic that my mother was largely absent from my life at that point. In fact, the last time I'd seen her was my junior year of high school.

After one of the countless moments of my life wasted on waiting for the train carrying my mother, the one that never came, I'd gotten my license. I could drive and had a phone number allowing me to keep in contact with my mother. But still, I never saw her. Finally, I called my mother to tell her I'd gotten my license. The phone rang on and on and on before someone picked up, a blaring roar the first thing in my ear. Apparently, there was some kind of house party happening. I could hear music thumping and people laughing and shouting, trying to get my mother to the phone.

She was laughing, I remember that. I, on the other hand, had reached my limit. I told her not to call me again until she was sober, and she didn't. True to her word, she stayed the fuck out of my life until I was a junior in college. Even now, after years of healing, it still baffles my mind how fucked up it was that she just disappeared when I needed her most.

ꙮ 6 ꙮ

FATHER FIGURE

By now, you're probably wondering where my father was in all of this. I still wonder that, too. James Kilpatrick met my mother in New York where both were heavy into the "Fight the Power" movement. My father was actually a leader in the anti-racist campaign at Northeastern University, despite the fact that he was and still is predominantly white.

His whiteness was something he didn't always acknowledge, which made my growing up as a biracial child even more challenging given the odd messages I was receiving. My father was incredibly opinionated on race issues and how people of color, "like him," had been consistently marginalized throughout history.

At some point, my father had traced his ancestry back and learned that a great grandfather was Cape Verdean. From that moment, my father cemented himself - falsely in my opinion - as a person of color, even though his ancestry is largely white and nothing about his appearance says otherwise.

To this day, he has no understanding that just by being a man and having pale skin he was already ahead of the game. He has never been stopped by the police simply for having dark skin. He has never had anyone question his qualifications or his belonging somewhere because of his skin color. That he insisted on identifying with people having much darker skin, and far more negative experiences in life, was confusing to me, though we did have some powerful conversations about race and identity.

But I needed a father and that was definitely an area in which he was sorely lacking. I needed warmth and guidance, boundaries and insight. Instead, I felt like another person he was trying to sway into agreeing with his opinions. When someone, including me, didn't agree, he went into victim mode, living his life like a traumatized individual that never got what he felt entitled to. I know now there was no real way to parent from that mindset, but in my childhood it just hurt. It still does. He sits so comfortably in his victimhood and it drives me fucking crazy.

As previously mentioned, in the aftermath of my parents' divorce, my father married Maggie, who became my stepmother, though never in a way that seemed like enough for her. While having her around was helpful during the more difficult times with my mother, there seemed to be a dynamic between Maggie and I and my mother in which Maggie never felt as though she was enough. If I wasn't constantly gushing over her or heaping praise on her in order to feed her ego, it was easily bruised.

For example, during a visit to my old apartment in Brookline, Maggie noticed that there weren't any photos of her and I together. I can't remember why I didn't have any, but it wasn't intentional. Regardless, Maggie had a dramatic emotional reaction to the absence of said photo and the perceived slight, taking it deeply personally even though it wasn't at all personal.

The relationship between my father and Maggie confused me immensely. Although my father was supposed to be all for feminism and honoring women as powerful people, he treated Maggie with condescension and derision, often yelling at her and belittling her. I spent a lot of time trying to protect her from my father. I'd stand up to him, demanding that he not speak to her like that, but she would defend him and make excuses for his behavior. It was a pattern that kept repeating.

My father was a psychotherapist and is a professor at a small college, teaching classes on racism and diversity. I'm sure that few of his colleagues know that he had an affair with a client. Though I believe they ended their professional relationship, he was in an active affair with the woman for five years and chose to involve me in it, bringing me to her house on occasion to hang out. He was still married to Maggie, but here I was witnessing him making out with this other woman. When I asked him why he'd do something like that and bring me along, he told me, "If I die, I want someone to know that she was important to me." What?! All I could think, can still think, was how completely messed up that was.

The day after he'd brought me with him to the woman's house, I'd had enough. I told him that if he didn't tell Maggie, I would, as she deserved to know and his actions weren't fair to her or to me.

For a while, he and Maggie separated, and eventually divorced. When they told me they were getting back together, it was the conversation about the other woman that replayed through my mind on repeat. I was dumbfounded. Technically, it was none of my business. It was theirs, but I couldn't let it go. The second my father involved me he'd made it my business.

Later, when I was living in Jamaica Plain, during a period when my dad and Maggie were "on" again, I was out at a local bar with friends when he walked in with the other woman. My jaw dropped. I turned to one of my friends and asked her if the woman had waist-length blonde hair. When she said yes, I gasped.

"That's the fucking woman!" I hissed.

I walked past and said nothing, but definitely made him aware of my presence. I refused to leave "my" bar. He was the invader. When I returned to my seat, he came by and tried sharing a joke, playing down the situation. I wasn't having it and asked him if Maggie knew he was at the bar with his "special friend." He shrugged it off and went back to his table.

Soon, he was back and begging me not to say anything. I refused.

"I would really appreciate it if you would behave better," I sneered.

Back at my apartment, I called people I trusted and discussed the situation, ultimately deciding to tell Maggie. He should have been smart enough to confess but didn't. When he tried arguing with me about telling Maggie the truth, I shut him down, unwilling to become part of his lies. I told her he'd been with her, obviously having an afternoon together.

When I was a teen growing up in my father's house, there seemed to be no end to our conflict, which often arose over petty issues, such as the time I left a single dish in the sink and was later met with a pile of dirty dishes left on my bed. My father decided I wasn't doing enough to help out and the dishes were his passive-aggressive way of saying so. But what I needed was for my father to have a little perspective on all that I'd endured thus far with my mother (and him), and that my not washing a dish wasn't exactly the biggest fucking deal in the world at the moment.

Sometime during my high school years, my father made me attend a group for kids with alcoholic parents and also put me in therapy. The group helped some since it was good to talk with kids in similar situations, but seeing their pain was incredibly difficult. Parental addiction is a really challenging thing to talk about, and watching these kids share their pain was heartbreaking, and part of the reason I didn't end up attending for very long. I had my own heartache. I couldn't bear adding more.

I also needed more from Maggie where he was concerned. I believe this is why I've gotten so annoyed when Maggie chooses not to interfere or intervene when my father is on a tear. She claims she intervened many times in an attempt to protect me, but decided at some point that it wasn't her place. I never understood why that was okay. She witnessed him hurting me emotionally, and where she once stepped in, she now stepped back.

Making matters worse was the fact that my brother was treated entirely differently. I can't imagine what Maggie's reaction might be if my father spoke to him the way he does to me. My guess is she'd do everything in her power to protect Ian in order to show him that she loves him. That's what parents do. They stand up for their children. Even their stepchildren. Why not me? The message I received was that perhaps I simply wasn't worth enough. Whether intended or not, it certainly felt that way. Intentions have shown me a whole lot of nothing in this lifetime. To me, they're emptier than promises.

Truth is, I love Maggie, for many reasons. She did step in. She did fill a role, and she's a great mother to Ian. She does wonderful work with children. She even got a handle on her own addiction when I came to live with her. We never spoke much about it, but I wish we had.

Before she was with my father, before I was aware of their relationship, their affair, she was an amazing babysitter. I would go down to her classroom where she'd let me hang out and give me treats and activities to do. She'd worked with teen mothers for years, as well as recovering addicts, and was deeply caring and thoughtful in that work. I lie awake at night wondering how this chasm between us grew so wide that she doesn't even have a connection with my daughter, whom she hasn't spoken with in some time. She'll say that's how I wanted it. While that's partly true, I made that decision during a period of time in which it was immensely clear that it was the only choice.

After we all attended therapy together, I gave our relationship my best effort. I hoped that she and my father were too. My dad does talk with Blessing once a week as part of a new tradition that's still unfolding. I just wish often that it was different. Less strained.

I want Maggie, her friends, and even people I know to understand that her being there when my mom wasn't didn't go unnoticed. It wasn't taken for granted, but at some point, I was. No matter how well you fill in for an absentee parent, it should never be conditional. Love is not something that ought to come with conditions. I get that Maggie wanted to be my friend and as part of that, wanted me to call her all the time. But she was never my friend in the same way I will never be "friends" with my stepsons, Holden and Sean. They are my family first. I am a parent first. Perhaps because of Maggie's own troubled upbringing, she didn't learn this, but given how things went with Ian, I believe she figured it out. I just wish things were better between us.

The same goes for my father. The challenge is that when I think of him I am alternately impressed, disgusted, and disappointed, mostly with his decision not to be a better father. He does care. I know this. It is because of him that I am the passionate activist I am. He, along with my mother, taught me invaluable lessons about policy, politics, race, and the importance of fighting for what's right whenever possible, though I think my mom's afro could have done that on its own.

In many ways, he made it possible for white people to become allies, to learn the steps they could take in changing race relations. So, what's the problem? My father's relationship with his biracial daughter. If you can't create love within your own home as an example of how you'd lead others, your work just seems worthless and empty. He was simply never healed enough to be the parent I needed, especially when my mother was gone, unable to fully understand intimacy, ego, trauma, strong emotions and the connection between them all. He often says to me, "Due to my trauma as a kid, I just wasn't able to be the parent to you I should have been."

I call bullshit. I could use the same excuse where I'm concerned, writing off my relationship with Blessing by attributing my bad parenting to my mother's addictions and actions. But I made a conscious choice to do the opposite, a choice I make every day. Some days it's as easy as getting out of bed. Others, it's a struggle, but it is the work I am most proud of as a parent. It is how I remain present for her, helping her know that by the energy I bring, the spirit that surrounds us.

7

THAT FIRST BUZZ

When I was in high school, I was vehemently against drinking. While other kids were out sowing their proverbial wild oats and doing who knows what, I was doing my best to stay well clear of all of it. I was determined not to become my mother.

But once I got to college I was like, "Let me try this." I remember my friends and I being at some club somewhere in Boston. As I'd always loved to dance, I was out on the dance floor, my first-ever buzz ebbing slowly through my body, which felt light and free. At the moment, I had no idea about what I was getting myself into. I just knew that I felt amazing and danced with no inhibitions, free as a bird soaring in a clear blue sky.

In the beginning, my drinking was under control, balanced between classes and studying. But the seeds of addiction had been planted and were gradually taking root, silently whispering to me that this, that drinking, was my ticket out of all the pain I felt.

When it came to comparisons with my mother, that addiction voice was clever, repeating often that I wasn't anything like her. I had *my* drinking under control, unlike my mother and her constant alcohol-and-drug-fueled drama. That voice was helped in delivering its insidious messages by my already low self-esteem, which reminded me constantly that I'd only gotten into college because I'd written a good essay, not because I was intelligent enough to handle it.

Ironically, I was doing amazingly well academically. I was a top student, earning high marks on my work, my essays on racism and diversity added to the college library so that others could read them and begin to understand the race issue from the perspective of a black/biracial woman. They received high praise and I felt respected, empowered, and as though I was making a genuine difference in the world.

And yet, I was still drinking, more frequently and in greater amounts. I knew that if anything went wrong in my life, alcohol would take it away, my brain finally making that fateful connection between the drug and my happiness, putting into place the final puzzle piece to my alcoholism.

After graduating from Wheelock, I plummeted. Like a sailboat adrift with no rudder, I was well and truly lost. I attribute my downfall to my mother's return into my life. She'd reentered during my junior year of college. I recall my friends being deeply confused, having believed - based on what I'd told them - that she was dead. She wasn't, but since my mother had burned every bridge, sabotaged every relationship, and left in her wake a trail of people that disliked her, ours was the relationship she clung to and I eagerly assumed the role of her caretaker. I had no idea that her coming back into my life would erase all of the goodness I'd built into my world, wiping it all away and taking me back to that place of fear and desperation I'd existed in constantly as a child.

From the moment we reconnected during a surreal meeting at the CambridgeSide Galleria, I became trapped in her orbit, spiraling away from the determined college graduate I was. I didn't even consider the impact of becoming, essentially, her sponsor. Any semblance of a mother-daughter relationship was nonexistent, but since she wasn't "independently sober," or able to stay sober on her own, being her go-to person fell to me.

The problem was that although my mother had allegedly stopped drinking, she hadn't begun to heal. She might not have been drinking, but neither was she going to any kind of meeting, treatment facility, or even a therapist. She called Alcoholics Anonymous "Adventures and Assholes" and refused to go. She didn't believe in god and was in a regular mood of bitterness and anger. She was basically still a drunk, but without the booze.

When you're in your twenties, you're not fully grown. You're still so close to adolescence, even if you've been out in the wider world thanks to work or schooling. In that youthful mindset it was easy to fall back into the patterns of codependent angst with my mother. Of feeling like a child whose duty it was to take care of her. That was my job. Anything getting in the way of my ability to do that job was the enemy. From the moment of her return until the day she died more than 10 years later, that was my MO, my driving force, even as I ignored the anxiety-fueled adrenaline coursing through my veins almost constantly.

All of the support fell on me, and I, desperate as I was for whatever mothering I could find, suddenly regressed to the child I had been, ready to do whatever I could to keep my mother in my life, my decision fueled by all of those moments I sat waiting for the train that never came. Thank god I could escape into a bottle of wine whenever I needed to.

❀ 8 ❀

HALF BREED

I had more than five outfit changes to make that night. The blonde wig and the skintight white, high-heel, zip-up, over-the-knee boots were the most difficult to get into. While I worked on a zipper, I could hear my mother as she simultaneously smoked cigarettes and ripped my father a new asshole.

It was my 30th birthday. The "save the date" cards had gone out four months prior. As I'd been born in 1973, the theme of the party was the 1970s, with the title "Bringing it Back." My five best girlfriends, my roommates, some grad school buddies, and I had planned the party of the century, which included a DJ, and catering by Roche Brothers. My outfits were ready. The party was soon to start. I wanted to be ready, too.

"Who the FUCK does he think he is anyway?" My mother shouted from the porch in her raspy, smoked-out, chesty voice.

The struggle was real.

The struggle was my love-hate relationship with my mother and it was so real that I couldn't wish it away no matter what I did, or how much I drank. As I tried focusing my attention on the impending celebration of my life, I tried ignoring her screeching.

Soon, the drinks were flowing as guests in funky costumes poured into the party, disco lights flashing and further enhancing the scene. I surreptitiously snuck my younger brother and his girlfriend drinks. Twelve years younger than me, he used to call my mother the "brown mommy" since he and I shared the same father, but had different mothers.

In what seemed like no time at all, there were more than 100 people dancing and singing, everyone getting sweaty as they grooved, marveling at each outfit change I presented, every one offering a tribute to a different aspect of the 70s. My costume designer had planned each reveal perfectly in keeping with the flow of the evening, the outfits getting tighter and skimpier as the evening went on.

As a fun gift, someone had stationed a time capsule box into which people could put gifts, which I'd look at during the party, then put away for a decade, to be opened again when I turned 40. I couldn't wait to see what inside that box was so crazy cool. What's that phrase? Be careful what you wish for?

There was a time when my parents were powerfully bonded, having met in New York City, both fully immersed in the Civil Rights protests of the 1960s, connecting over strife and black inequality. They each had their own reasons for fighting the powers that were, but on my 30th birthday, and for the previous 25 years, my mother detested my father. Loathed him, and not in a small way. She hated him as if her soul depended upon it.

She would tell anyone that would listen story after story of what he'd done and what he still did that made him such a wretched person. She was already difficult to argue with, but when it came to my father, you had no choice but to nod with conviction and nervous laughter.

"Fuckin' Jimmy!" She'd shout.

Her language and tone were such that it was difficult to tell when she was kidding or serious, the listener always hoping for the former.

"What a prick!" She said, a cigarette dangling from her mouth, a good-sized ash already forming on the tip, no drink in her hand this time. She was stone-cold sober and still crass as hell.

It was time for the time capsule contents to be revealed. My friends read rhyming poems, roasting me about my fabulous drinking habits, which I didn't find all that funny but was glad that others could still laugh at. Then came Cher.

No. Not the actual person. Nor was there an impersonator. But I digress. Before telling you about Cher, let me explain something else about my father and I. Unlike many father-daughter teams, we didn't have a special song or our own dance. We didn't have a movie or a sport or anything that belonged to just the two of us as so many fathers and daughters did. About the only commonality we had was that we both liked to dance, though not always with each other, which makes the Cher incident that much more humiliating.

As I looked around the party, I noticed that pieces of paper with typed-up writing on them were being hastily passed around. I couldn't read what was on them, but it looked like song lyrics. When the singing began, it felt as if the walls were closing in on me as panic set in. To say that I was mortified would be a massive understatement and doesn't do the moment justice.

> *"Half-breed, that's all I ever heard*
> *Half-breed, how I learned to hate that word*
> *Half-breed, she's no good they warned*
> *Both sides were against me since the day I was born."*

My father was singing Cher's autobiographical song "Half-Breed" at my 30th birthday celebration, about me. Suddenly, among the song's chorus, which some in the crowd had begun to sing along with, came my mother's screech.

"He can't be fucking serious!" She hissed. "Jimmy! Shut up! Turn that shit off you idiot! What's wrong with you?"

My father continued belting out the offensive lyrics while everyone else, even my friends, chimed in at the chorus, his fist pumping as he urged everyone to sing louder and louder. I begged a friend next to me to please get me a drink. Or five. Anything to make it stop. Unfortunately, I wasn't nearly drunk enough to find his performance even remotely funny.

My father thought he was giving me the greatest gift of all time, not seeing how utterly inappropriate the song and his singing it was. The inappropriateness was even lost on the crowd of people that he continued to egg on before the song finally ended and the lyrics were, astonishingly, put into the time capsule for me to look back on. To this day, I still have PTSD whenever my father gets up to speak about or do something for his children, terrified of the humiliation that could follow.

Before the song ended, my mother continued ordering him to stop, as if just saying so would make it happen. It didn't, but even though her comments and chatter were simply part of the general background party noise by then, they were all I wanted to hear in that moment. For the first time in my adult life, her voice was comforting. But what made it that much better was looking for my mother after the song ended, my father's torment complete. My eyes found hers as she stood, proudly, giving my father the middle finger. And me? I couldn't help but smile.

✣ 9 ✣

GUS

While I was in college, I had a boyfriend named August. He went by Gus and, like my friend Emily, taught me what unconditional love really felt like.

Gus was the most grounded person I've ever met. It's possible he still is. He was compassionate, funny, and handsome as hell. His green eyes went on for days. Aside from Emily, he was the closest person to my mother. He never judged her, not even when he saw her nearly at her worst. I'd never seen anything like it. It was beautiful and amazing, and a bit surreal.

The first time he met her she was pretty tipsy. She'd just come back into my life and he was the only one I'd really spoken to about her before her return. My college friends were still under the impression that my mother had mysteriously died one day.

After my fateful meeting with my mother at the Cambridge-Side Galleria, where she swore she'd never drink again as per the conditions of being in my life, the next time I saw her was at a dinner she hosted at her apartment to which I brought Gus. She was frantically preparing food when we arrived, her cheeks flushed and the small space growing increasingly warm. I knew immediately she'd been drinking.

I was painfully embarrassed. I looked at Gus and hung my head in disappointment as he flashed me a smile. As if he knew very well how to diffuse such a bomb, he engaged her in conversation, winning her over with his charming personality, making her laugh. The two were inseparable after that, brought into her inner circle as one of the few people who could see who she was without her bullshit. It wasn't lost on me that she didn't try giving him any guff back.

If Gus hadn't been there that night, I doubt I'd have ever seen my mother again. She'd broken our agreement, and I didn't take that lightly. But he had a way of talking with me about the situation that didn't excuse her behavior, but instead met it with empathy. She'd been nervous. Not mean. She was trying, and she was an alcoholic.

As we left her place after dinner, I held Gus's hand on the way out, his squeeze in return letting me know I wasn't alone.

When she was sad and struggling and couldn't reach me, she'd often reach out to Gus. They'd go to the movies or he'd take her to run errands. She loved him and he was the best friend I'd ever had. He was the only one in the world I trusted fully, and the only person who knew every part of me, including my mother.

Sadly, as time went on and I lost more and more of myself, I lost him, too. The more I drank in my attempts to distance myself from who I was, the worse I treated Gus, until he reached his limit and left. His departure will always be one of my biggest regrets, for it was Gus who let me know what real love was like.

❧ 10 ❧

ON GUARD

I watched her sleep. I could never tell whether she was breathing or not, so I'd try getting as close to her as possible without waking her, inching my feet across the floor toward her. I just wanted to feel her breath. As I shuffled ever so quietly, so as not to startle her, I narrowed my eyes to focus on the blanket draped across her to see if it was moving with the rise and fall of her chest. Was she breathing? The television was on, god-awful infomercials featuring over-the-top hucksters trying to convince foolish night owls to buy their cheap goods, the coffee table littered with empty bottles of booze.

Most nights, I'd confirm that my mother was, indeed, breathing, but it was so shallow and sporadic, sometimes coming in hitches and fits, that I was terrified that if I left her for even a moment, or closed my own eyes, that her breath would get stuck and stop altogether. I prayed that I be allowed to breathe with her, and maybe that way I could keep her alive, with me, for one more night. I was seven years old and the taste of my fear was metallic in my mouth.

Looking back now, not long after my daughter turned that very age, I am aware that was the moment that I truly understood what raw, gut-wrenching fear felt like.

The first time I ever saw my mother drunk was at a holiday party when I was six. I didn't know what "drunk" was, but somehow I understood that the more of whatever she drank, the scarier things got. I remember the pained expressions on the faces of other partygoers, who would pat me on the head or my back in gestures of hollow sympathy.

After a while, my mother could barely speak, her eyes open a mere fraction. A cab was called and an attempt was made to put her and I inside, but it was cold and icy and my mother fell multiple times, laughing so hard at something that definitely didn't seem at all humorous. I remember looking up at the adult that closed the taxi door once we were finally inside with what I'm sure was a pleading expression on my little face, but she simply shook her head and walked away.

That's when I learned that just because someone is an adult, even a parent, doesn't ensure that they will always keep you safe, no matter how much they love you.

A short while later, and after much maneuvering my nearly inert mother from the cab into our apartment, I had resumed my position, staring intently at my mother as I made certain she was breathing. This, I was keenly aware now, was how it was going to be, and if I wanted to keep her with me, my job was to keep her alive, regardless of how painful each agonizing night was, no matter how much it felt like I was a hamster trapped on a wheel I wasn't spinning.

11

BEREFT

On September 13, 2008, my mother died. Three days prior, I'd gotten a startling but not-unexpected call. "Is this Yani?" Sheila asked. She was the manager of my mother's apartment complex.

"Yes, how can I help you?" I asked warily.

"It's your mom," Sheila sighed. "She's fallen again. This time we found her on the sidewalk with her tank." The frustration in Sheila's voice was evident.

My mother was a hoarder and smoked at least a pack of cigarettes a day in spite of the full-blown emphysema that was killing her with every inhale of the noxious chemicals into her lungs, and in spite of her being attached to an oxygen tank. This was something the complex management had just figured out. *Took you long enough.* I thought. How they didn't know was beyond me. My guess is they simply didn't want to acknowledge it.

"We called an ambulance," Sheila continued. "She's at the hospital." She paused. "I'm sorry, Yani. She just can't come back here."

"Well, it's about time!" I all but barked. "Are you going to tell her that?"

There was a long silence at the other end of the phone. It dawned on me that each person that had come into contact with Ms. Valerie Lake was, in some way, afraid of her. Except this time I wasn't willing to accept the brunt of the anger as I had for so long. I was so tired of it. But in the end, it would again fall on me.

"I'm kidding," I said in a tight voice even though it was the most unfunny thing ever.

Sheila hung up.

I called the hospital to let them know I was on my way and to speak with her primary care physician. What a truly wonderful woman to have dealt so well with my mother as she had been then. She'd been swept up in my mother's charm, as had all the cute young male assistants, hospital workers, and personnel. Every time she was admitted for more than a day, she would convince all of those young men to wheel her up to the roof in her wheelchair to "look at the view." Then they'd let her smoke on the roof, out of sight of her doctors and nurses, who seemed none the wiser. She was sneaky, to say the least.

"I think we might be at the right place to move forward," her doctor told me with a heavy sigh.

"With the paperwork? I can finally sign it? You'll actually let me this time?" I was half frustrated and half relieved, neither of which sat well with me.

"Yes. I don't think we have a choice this time," she replied.

My mother was the definition of fiercely independent. She refused to allow me, or anyone at all for that matter, make a single decision for her. She refused everything - any medication that might help her, talking with anyone that could support her... she refused it all.

She'd needed to be in a nursing home far sooner than this and the hospital agreed, but my mother did not, and since her mind was sharp enough to allow her to make her own decisions, there was nothing the hospital could do except send her home and wait, sadly, for her return.

I was impressed with their consideration of patient rights, but the result was continued misery and an almost unbearable sense of being. That said, I took comfort in knowing that her doctor had not wavered at all on certain requirements and emphasized that while she disagreed with my mother's refusal to move into a safer environment, respected her decision to return to her apartment.

My mother took note of that and treated the doctor with similar respect in return, offering harcore loyalty and transparent honesty. Except for the rooftop visits, that is.

Now, things were different. On this day I was finally given the go-ahead to become her healthcare proxy and make difficult decisions for her as she was no longer able to make them herself. I was so relieved that she'd finally be getting properly cared for in a safe environment, and at the same time my heart was breaking at having to rob this once-powerful woman of her independence, not to mention challenging her feminist values.

Still on the phone, I was put through to the nurses. "It's Valerie's daughter," I said. "I'm on my way." No response. They were talking to each other in the background as if I couldn't hear them.

"It's the daughter. What should we say?" One of the nurses said in a hushed tone as she tried unsuccessfully to cover the mouthpiece of the phone.

Fuck. I thought, suddenly cold. *Maybe* this *is the time?*

Then I remembered that we'd been at this moment multiple times in the past two months. She *wasn't* dying.

"She's been unresponsive for a while now," the nurse said softly. "No vital signs. This really could be it. You shouldn't come alone."

Are you KIDDING ME? It's for real this time?

My thoughts raced faster than I could catch up. I wondered how it was they knew that *this* time was different than all the other times when they'd told me the same thing? Overwhelmed, I called my best friend and told her I needed a favor.

"Happy birthday," Emily said. I'd forgotten it was my birthday until that moment. I glanced at the calendar on my wall. September 9th. Yup. Suddenly, I realized I'd forgotten who I was.

Empty was a step up from where my emotions were by then, and I was jealous of those who felt empty. I was nothing more than a shell of a human, clinging to the barest threads of hope, willing myself to breathe in and breathe out, to just fucking survive.

"Thanks," I mumbled. "I need you to come with me to the hospital. They are convinced that this is it and told me not to come alone." It was the fifth time that month she'd heard those words from me.

"Are you sure?" She asked.

I frowned, frustrated and scared. "Who the fuck knows?" I said. "But I have to go find out, right? I'm sorry to do this to you again."

"I will see you soon," she said softly.

I was not allowed to go into my mother's room until Emily arrived. I peeked in and the sight startled me. There were wires everywhere, going in and coming out of myriad places. Her skin seemed to be dripping off of her body. I had never seen her so thin. She was a 63-year-old woman going on 95. I thought of all those experiences and choices that stacked on top of each other and weathered her skin and toughened her mind. Tougher still was her will, carrying her through all those years of cocaine, booze, drugs and pain.

I felt a mix of horror and deep respect for her when I thought about her experiences in the world. I tried to hate her, but then images of her as a little girl in the New York school library, teaching herself. She'd survived constant abuse, rape, and who knows what else. The bottom line was that she was incredibly brave. So very brave. And now it was just the two of us trying to coexist in this world together, and she was dying.

Memories swirled through my mind: Picnics by the Charles River when we lived in Cambridge where we'd have "heart-to-hearts" as she called them, just us girls telling each other everything. The sun would begin to set and I would get sad that we'd need to go inside and the moment would end.

Night brought uncertainty. I was never sure what would happen after dark, whether it would be peaceful or fearsome, and because of this I clung to those moments when I felt safe and loved, wanting to hold them close to me always. When night came, I was terrified of what would happen to her when I went to sleep.

Now, here I was at 35, staring at the shiny white tile of the hospital floor on my 35th birthday. I was struck by the realization that since I was six years old, I'd gone to bed filled with fear at not knowing whether my mother would actually wake up again. It seemed the day had arrived when she truly wouldn't.

Emily finally made it to the hospital, somehow looking more tired than I was. "Ready?" The nurse asked us. "You can talk to her but we're not sure what she's taking in at this point."

I was all of a sudden furious. I was so angry with my mother, and with myself for giving her all of me for what felt like no good reason. She had never really been a good mother. Was never a real mother, for that matter, not that I had any idea what that meant, but I knew that I was always more of an adult than she was. I knew I had given too much of myself to her to ever get it back in this lifetime. I was exhausted. I was angry. And she was dying.

Her frail body and the bed that seemed to be swallowing her were propped upright to allow for better circulation and breathing. Wires attached to various machinery searched for any change in her vital signs. The hospital seemed eerily silent.

"Mom? It's me. Can you hear me?" I asked, my tone nearly as cold as the hospital felt.

More silence. No one moved. It felt as if the entire lobby was watching. I closed my eyes and attempted to draw in a breath when I heard the scratchiest, most sarcastic voice ever.

"Hey kid, did you think I was going to die on your birthday?" My mother bellowed with a hearty laugh, followed by a cough, the laugh belying her frailty.

That fucking bitch. I couldn't believe it. Everyone was in shock and laughing awkwardly. The faces of the nurses looked as if they'd seen the funniest ghost in all the world. Two of the cute young black men, probably the ones that had been taking her on her rooftop field trips, were high fiving each other in the background. Two other nurses that had been through it all simply shook their heads and stalked away, utterly annoyed and more than a little peeved.

Only my mother could frustrate them by *not* dying. Only my mother could rise from the dead to make an off-color joke like that. That she wasn't dead and hadn't died baffled medical professionals, who flocked to her room in disbelief.

"Get away from me you stupid people! Let my kid through. It's her birthday," she said sternly, scolding them all. I waved goodbye to Emily, who headed to the parking garage, her head and shoulders heavy with the exhaustion that Valerie and Ayanna tended to foster.

I spent my 35th birthday in the hospital next to my mother, where I stationed myself for the night, caught in that familiar lifelong tangle of fear and security. Fear because it was clear that I was losing her, security because she was still there.

This was the woman who gave me life. Who brought me into this world and taught me so much, but also abandoned me and hurt both of us deeply. This was the woman I constantly feared would not come back to me, would leave me for good.

Now that I had the power to make decisions regarding my mother's care, the first thing I did was add Ativan to her daily medication regimen. The second was to find her a nursing home. Lord bless whatever home this woman was going to end up in, for they wouldn't have an easy time of things. I had to be strategic. I couldn't look like, smell like, or sound like a nursing home, a tall order if you're at all familiar with actual nursing homes, particularly those for people with little to no funds.

I left the hospital and was soon in my car, sweating bullets as I hoped to find a place in time. Lately it seemed that my life was full of sweats born of panic, fear, regret, or desperation, not to mention the physical toll that alcohol was taking on my body.

Frantically, I drove around Winthrop and East Boston, racing, searching, desperate and frightened, but also hopeful. Most of the homes I visited were nothing short of disgusting, full of once proud individuals reduced to nothing more than human zombies, slumped into their wheelchairs. But there was one that stood out. The Lighthouse.

My mother loved the beach. She loved the islands, particularly Martha's Vineyard, and anyplace with a lighthouse. My eyes filled with tears as I walked slowly up the front steps, praying hard that this would be the one. A woman walked out smiling. *She was someone's daughter,* I told myself. *She was visiting her mother and just had a wonderful visit.*

The director met me at the door, greeting me with a smile. I shook her hand and noticed that while my body felt heavy with exhaustion, it also felt lighter than it had in some time. I'd finally found a home, for both of us. My mother would be safe and well cared for and I would be able to let her go and hopefully find some peace in that.

The trick was getting her there. It would take cunning, and I needed everyone in on the ruse. We couldn't miss a beat. No one could be a weak link or Valerie would know. I smiled to myself as I made my way along the hospital hallway toward her room, eager to share the news and get the plan in place when I heard my mother's voice.

"It's a goddamn conspiracy!" She shouted in her raspy voice. "He's trying to drug me! Get the hell away from me!"

Not again. And not today. I fought the urge to turn and run. My mother was on numerous steroids to keep her lungs functioning even slightly, but a major side effect was that her behavior frequently became psychotic and irrational. Because the steroids were essentially the reasons she could breathe at all, there was nothing I could do to take her off them.

I was turning around when Emily appeared. Somehow, she was always there. "Hey," she said. "I've got this."

Judging by the sounds coming from my mother's room, objects were now being thrown. Emily, meanwhile, walked confidently into the eye of Hurricane Val. "Hi Val. It's Em," she said.

"Do you see that stupid white *murse*?" My mother hissed, using a derogatory slang term to describe a male nurse. "He needs to go fuck with someone else. He is part of the conspiracy to drug me, Em! He is trying to kill me! What is wrong with him? Leave, you fucking idiot!"

My mother continued shouting as Emily calmly walked to her side, far more calmly than I would have had the patience to do, and my mother began to quiet down.

Frustrated to the point of bursting, I stormed into the room in full on Hurricane Ayanna mode. "There is no goddamn conspiracy Mom! Je-SUS! Why do you have to do this every freaking time?" I was practically screaming. The poor nurse was shaking. "Sorry," I said, turning to him. Emily was quietly asking my mother about the conspiracy and what she thought Obama was going to do when he found out. That was the magic word - Obama. My mother loved that man and knew he was going to be president. It was so important for her to see that happen after all that she had fought for in the 1960s, armed with her afro and her fist.

Soon, Emily and Val were lost in a conversation on politics and planning the welcome party for Barack Obama when suddenly I had an idea. *That's it!* I thought. There was the ticket into the nursing home: a welcome party.

While Emily continued distracting my mother, I gathered the nurses together and told them the plan was to get Valerie to Lighthouse. They were enthusiastically in, and together we huddled, a madcap football team with a uniform mainly consisting of white coats, scrubs and clogs, and I was their quarterback, calling the plays and assigning the various roles. All that was missing was the whiteboard with Xs and Os on it.

The head nurse called her friends at a local fire department and arranged for the three most attractive EMTs to handle this very special transport. I was grateful when they were more than happy to oblige. I think everyone was secretly happy to watch my mother leave that way as opposed to the alternative we all thought would be the case, and which I was most afraid of.

While everyone was getting into position, I relayed the plan to Emily, who told my mother that she had to go but that the conspiracy had been taken care of and there was a party my mother had to get to. My mother smiled. She trusted Emily wholeheartedly and allowed herself some excitement, her face lighting up like a child's at Christmas. "For me?" she asked.

"Yup!" Emily replied. "Have fun!"

We needed to move quickly, our plan officially underway. After kissing my mother on the forehead, Emily blew me a kiss of my own and it occurred to me that Emily was far more mature than both my mother and I together. Thankfully.

As arranged, three strapping young EMTs, confident and distracting in their crisp uniforms, swooped in, all smiles as they greeted my mother with charm and kindness. The nurses had prepared them well.

"Val! We heard you had a big party to get to!" One of the men said as they kept moving her, strapping her onto the gurney, talking nonstop to avoid her questions. My mother went along for the ride, waving goodbye and inviting everyone to her party. The staff waved back, winking at me in the understanding that they would likely never see her again.

My grief threatened to bring me to my knees, but I couldn't show anything and risk her figuring things out. Once in the elevator, the three EMTs still smiling at my mother, she turned up the humiliation dial.

"My daughter is single, you know," she said as I cringed inwardly. "You are all invited to the party. She needs some lovin'. Leaving her would be easier if I knew she had some lovin'." My mother smiled her Cheshire Cat smile at them.

Meanwhile, I was purple from embarrassment, secretly hoping the elevator floor would open and I'd fall through. The elevator suddenly felt stifling and I realized that in the hubbub of trying to maintain the charade, I'd forgotten that I was claustrophobic. I couldn't get the words "leaving her" out of my mind. They seemed to ricochet off the walls of the space.

We arrived at the nursing home without incident. It wasn't until we neared her room, the last she would ever occupy, that it finally dawned on her that there was no party. My mother was furious. As reality set in, she comprehended where she actually was, waiting for the staff to leave the room before tearing into me. I had taken away all of her strength, she told me, her honor, her dignity, herself. She acted like a tormented toddler in the throes of a major tantrum. It was akin to leaving your child at preschool for the first time, except the child wasn't simply sad and scared, but also goddam pissed and hated you for it.

She hated me for everything that night, especially after the nurse told her, "There's no smoking allowed in here, ma'am." In that moment, I became the sole reason for everything evil she had ever experienced, for every awful thing she had done in her lifetime, and oh man was she going to tell me all about it.

"I told you *not* to! Who the *fuck* do you think you are? What the hell is *wrong* with you? I *trusted* you! I hate you for doing this to me!" She kicked and screamed in fury, her tantrum never once subsiding. The nurses tried consoling me by explaining that such behavior was normal and that I could leave. This was something they dealt with all the time. But I didn't. I felt trapped.

Hospice arrived and met with my mother while I was signing the necessary paperwork, explaining that she was not a woman who was about to die. They told me I had time, that I didn't have to stay and should be back in touch with them when the time had arrived. In my mind, I laughed and thought, *she's already dead.* But I left. I left the screaming and the tantrum and retreated to the silence of my car.

I hastily found the closest liquor store, paid for a cheap box of wine and some plastic cups and returned to my car, where I sat in my back seat and cried, hugging my box of wine. It was not the first time I'd done this, but this was when the wine slowly began to replace any ideas I had about what real comfort looked like, the last of my self-love draining away with each drop I drank.

I fell asleep in my car, where I stayed the night, curled up in the back with my boxed wine and plastic cups, knowing I'd truly given up on myself. When I woke the next day, I prepared myself for the horror show I expected to walk into when I returned to her room. Instead, I found the opposite.

My mother looked beautiful, a stark contrast to my leftover, rumpled, bleary-eyed, spent-the-night-in-my-car appearance. She was in a brilliant white flowing bathrobe and pajamas. Her coffee skin was glowing. She was laughing with everyone as she discussed how she was going to go to karaoke that afternoon. WHAT?

"Oh, hey! You look like shit, kid, but it's nice to see you!"

I couldn't speak. The activities director was going down a list of all the things my mother could do and what she could eat, which was pretty much whatever she wanted, including all the ice cream she desired. She was happy and seemed at home, truly.

I relaxed my shoulders, trying to release some of the tension, and told her I was going home to shower and would be back soon. Except I didn't. That was the night I found myself at some Chinese restaurant, extremely drunk, waking up the next day with my phone in my hand and a slew of missed calls from the nursing home, as well as one from some man I didn't know.

Last I'd known, my mother was fine, shining bright. I'd rationalized that she was finally in a safe place, relieving me of worry, which had, however selfishly, felt good. I didn't have to be on high alert for once.

After my shower the previous day, I could have gone straight to the nursing home to be with her, but first indulged in a glass of wine while I was getting dressed. That glass turned into another and soon I was looking at myself in the mirror, horrified at myself and what I had become. That led to another glass of wine, and ultimately, the Chinese restaurant, after which I was oblivious to everything, including the repeated phone calls.

My mother, previously so vibrant and energetic as she welcomed her new home, had declined rapidly after I'd left. She'd had a wonderful day, but shortly after she'd gone to sleep, her body had begun to fail. Hospice had been called and they'd tried to reach me multiple times early that morning when it appeared that my mother was nearing her end.

Once again unshowered and looking horrendous, I got in my car and made the 45-minute trek back to the nursing home, begging and pleading with whatever god that existed to please let her hang on until I could get there. I called Emily on the way, hysterical, but not because my mother might finally be dying. Instead, I was ashamed at how badly I'd fucked up, passing out to the point where not even incessant phone calls could rouse me.

"I don't want to hear any of that right now," Emily said, ever supportive. "Just get to the hospital safely. I'll meet you there. Remember, you are human."

At the hospital, the hospice nurse was sitting in the rocking chair where I was supposed to be. Should have been.

"You were MIA for a while," she said, the same woman who three days prior had said my mother wasn't dying. Now, I wanted nothing more than to knock that smirk of judgment off her face, though I'm pretty sure my "after a night out" clothes and the stench of alcohol oozing out of my panic sweat helped validate that judgment.

I looked at my mother, a shell of herself in the bed.

"She doesn't have much longer," the nurse said.

"Like, how long are we talking?" I asked, not wanting the answer.

"A few hours, maybe more. Are you okay?" She asked, not referring to the current status of my mother's health. I didn't answer, but gently asked her to leave as I wanted to have my final moments with my mother by myself.

This, seemingly, was it. My mother was no joke. She was 100 percent correct when she said she wouldn't last one day in a nursing home. Her return to a near-death state seemed almost intentional. I guess she was ready to go. All of the staff came in to say goodbye and tell me what a pleasure she was to have there. I stared at them in disbelief. In a 24-hour period she had made a positive, loving impact on this community. She'd become the woman I always knew was in there, allowing herself to be present for those 24 hours. What a gift, for her, for them, and even for me.

Time slowed to a crawl. All the tubes and wires were gone from my mother's body. She was still breathing, but barely. I had no idea what on earth I was supposed to do. I stared vacantly out the window and thought about my mother telling me that she knew I was ready for her to go. I wanted to cry, to be sad, to be angry, but I just felt empty.

I remembered that I'd brought a CD player to the nursing home for her. I'd only brought one CD, Ruthie Foster.

> *"Ooh many a trials I have known*
> *Tryin' to give my children*
> *A happy home*
> *In times of trouble*
> *And tears from worry*

Woah I'm trying to keep my head held
Teach my feet not to be in such a hurry."

The lyrics from "Mama Said" lingered as I tried to piece together my sorrow over the impending loss and the complex emotions of what I wished she was and what I was actually losing, forever.

I let the song play as I sat by her bed, my head in her lap, my eyes closed. I vowed silently to myself to be better. To be better to myself. To be healthier. To be stronger, and to clean up my side of the street. I would quit drinking and go to the gym and do whatever yoga teachers did all day.

I felt more tired from mothering my mother in that moment than ever before, and as I pondered a future with myself as a mother, I decided that I shouldn't have children. I simply didn't have the energy to give to someone else, especially a child.

As my thoughts continued skipping through all the things I was going to do differently, all the ways I was going to plan my perfect future, I heard a strange sound coming from my mother's mouth. Off-white foam was dripping from her lips.

More petrified than I thought possible, I tried calling the nurse, but no sound came from my own mouth. I pushed the call button and the nurse appeared. I asked her what was happening.

"She's going, sweetheart," she said, softly. "That's just what happens to the body. I'll get a towel."

I put my hand on my mother's chest as Ruthie sang, "Woah mama said girl you better learn how to pray oh you got a soul a soul to save." The music bounced off the walls, a most fitting exit song, and I could see my mother's soul. It was as if all the bad things she'd ever done floated away and all that was left was her soul, right there atop my hand on her chest.

I watched as she took one last, ragged breath, the last of her life, and then she was gone. As I leaned down to kiss her cheek, the nurse returned and three of my friends burst into the room.

"She's gone," I told them. "But everything is taken care of. I need to leave. I just want to go out and I know a really good Chinese restaurant that will give us free drinks." I looked them squarely in the eye, giving them no other choice than to take me.

12

DROWNING IN ALCOHOL

After my mother died, I all but imploded. My drinking reached a new level of awful, and the place I found myself in was so dark not even a pinprick of light existed. I'd go out with a girlfriend or two for a liquid lunch, and there was always some odd understanding that I'd always drink far more than them, but no one really addressed the problem.

The messages I was receiving regarding my alcoholism were so conflicting, it was difficult to grasp the point. Someone would talk with me about my drinking, and then happily join me in a liquid lunch, drinking right along with me. Sometimes they'd even choose those moments to try and talk with me about my problem. In my head, I'd be thinking, "Why the fuck are you drinking *with* me then?"

After the aforementioned lunch with friends, during a time when I was pretty much couch surfing to get by, I went to a local bar and met up with a guy I knew through other acquaintances. I was already quite drunk and he didn't have the most upstanding motives, which, even in my drunkenness, I could somehow sense. But before long, I found myself in his car.

It dawned on me as we were speeding along the roadway that I shouldn't be in the car with him, suddenly aware that I was likely going to be attacked. Seeing no other way at the moment and in the state I was in, I literally flung open the car door and jumped out, somehow managing to roll away from the fast-moving car. The guy didn't even stop to see if I was all right.

How this wasn't rock bottom for me, I have no idea. As I walked, I'd stumble into bushes or trip over whatever was in my way, most often myself. I finally found my friend's house around 3 a.m. I must have looked like hell. My body was incredibly banged up, bruises everywhere, scratches from falling into the bushes, and scrapes from rolling out of a moving car. The concern on my friend's face was visible, but still not enough to wake me up. Not fully.

My friends urged me to get help as I clearly had a problem. But I wasn't ready to go to full-on rehab, so I went to day treatment and stopped drinking, at least during the time I was there. I even went to AA. It all lasted about six months. Then I met a guy I connected with who was pretty great and a lot of fun. We ended up going to New York City together. At the time, I felt like I was in good shape, maintaining my sobriety and exercising like crazy. Then, I fell off the wagon. Hard.

In a drunken state, though less so given that I'd only had three beers compared to my usual, which was far more, I went home with the guy, had sex with him, and got pregnant. As I didn't know right away, the guy and I continued seeing each other. It was really nice. Then, one day we went running and I couldn't run. I was exhausted and felt like I was going to pass out. It was very strange. I decided to go to the doctor, who ordered a pregnancy test. When the results came back, I called my best friend.

"This can't be," I told her.

She was mercifully understanding, and deeply saddened for me given how far it seemed I'd come beforehand.

The pregnancy was the catalyst for my return to drinking. While the guy was nice enough, he not only wasn't dad material, but neither was he anyone I wanted in my life on a permanent basis. Though I didn't tell him about the pregnancy, we ended up in a fierce argument soon after the positive test result, which gave me an excuse to sever ties. Soon after that, I got an abortion. I was grateful that such a procedure was available. I hadn't been raped or forced into the pregnancy but knew that I wasn't at all prepared for motherhood.

But it wasn't a decision I made lightly. I was not aloof about it. It would have put so much additional pressure on me then to bring a child into that world. I'm sure he or she would have been raised in the same awful dynamic I had been, filled with booze and chaos, conflict and endless excuses, and never-ending fear.

Once I'd made the decision to follow through with the procedure, it was incredibly difficult. I knew I was ending a life. I also knew that there could be a chance I might be able to care for the baby, but the truth was that there was a better chance that the baby would not be well taken care of at all at that point in my life. I couldn't even parent myself, let alone an infant who would rely upon me for everything. While I understood that abortion was the best choice, it didn't leave me unscathed. Never underestimate the emotional toll it can take on a woman's soul, forever.

Before you can have the procedure, you must be thoroughly checked out physically. I met with the doctor and noted that I'd been spotting a bit. The doctor decided to do an ultrasound to make sure everything was okay internally before performing the abortion. If something was wrong, they needed to know prior to the procedure.

I was sent to another office one floor down where they covered me, put cool jelly on my stomach, and swished it around with the handheld camera device. Suddenly, I could hear the heartbeat. I shut my eyes against the sound, as if that would dull it. I felt sick.

The technician, who apparently had no idea why I was really there, spun the screen in my direction and in a lilting, cheery voice said, "Take a look at your beautiful baby!"

Immediately, I burst into tears, which confused the technician until she checked her notes. "Oh shit. Shit," she said. "They didn't tell me this was an unwanted pregnancy. I am so sorry."

"I need to get off this fucking table right now," I grimaced through tears.

"Just give me one second to call upstairs," she replied, her voice almost a whisper.

Whatever she said into the phone didn't register with me at all. My body felt as though it had turned to icy stone. When the tech told me I could go, I watched as she left the room, then dressed and tried not to throw up, and not from morning sickness. I walked outside and into the frosty air of Brookline, the sidewalk cold and unyielding beneath my feet. I went straight to the closest liquor store.

I tried not to think about the fact that the tech really should have known, should have looked more carefully at my charts. I didn't want to see that screen. No way in hell did I want to look, and neither did I want to hear anything from the audio. I'd turned my head as far away as possible so as not to see, all the while blaming myself for getting pregnant. Apparently, the morning after pill doesn't always work.

The abortion added to my already massive guilt. It was a wise decision given where I was at in life but came with immense baggage. I remember waking up sobbing, unable to stop. I felt as if I'd done something truly horrible, unforgivable. It was the best decision I could have made then, but the ramifications were awful. Adding to the struggle was the awareness that I genuinely wasn't interested in that method of becoming a mother. In physically carrying a child and giving birth. The idea of something taking over my body for nine months horrified me, and once the procedure was done and I began feeling more like myself again, I decided to "celebrate."

That weekend I went out with a group of friends from one of my dance classes and just drank. I felt as if I was free even though I absolutely wasn't. For many nights, months and months worth, all I'd see when I'd close my eyes was that black-and-white screen, the bomp-bomp of the heartbeat in my ears, haunting me. I didn't want to want that baby. I knew that if I, for even one second, let that wanting in, I would never be able to let it go, let the baby go. Sometimes letting go is the bravest thing we can do.

While allowing a baby to occupy my body for nine months was unthinkable, allowing alcohol to rule my world constantly wasn't, though even now I'm not the kind of woman that would have enjoyed being pregnant. That said, I still have residual guilt about the experience. Every so often, I'll bleed for no apparent reason and I'm sure it's my body still attempting to detox from that trauma.

Aware that I had a problem, I continued to drink while also trying to control it, partly because I'd met Jason.

❧ 13 ❧

JASON

One of the highlights of life following graduate school was meeting my husband Jason. Technically, he's my second husband. Surprise! I was married once prior to a man named Dave, a kind, sweet, thoughtful person who was a real gentleman. But I wasn't ready. I'm still not sure that I'm ready to be married, even though I am. It always seems like a wonderful idea, especially when you're in love.

But addiction is hard. It's difficult to talk about, and at 29, when I was with Dave, I wasn't ready to even begin acknowledging that booze was an issue. Though it was painful to separate, it was necessary and I'm glad we did. I think of him fondly, and keep close to my heart the happy memories of laughter and joy.

Then came Jason. But first there was Edie. My friend Edie was a hoot. We worked together ages ago at a restaurant in Jamaica Plain, eventually becoming roommates to share the high cost of living in Boston.

Edie and I drank a lot together. We enabled each other to keep drinking in spite of concerns that it was excessive. I had just completed graduate school and was working at The Match Charter School in Brookline with a young man named Geoffrey Douglas, a tall, smart, Black youth who was ready for a change. Ready to become somebody new. He and I spent a lot of time talking about what that change would look like.

I was on my way home from a dance class when I received the devastating news: Geoffrey had been shot and killed on a train as many of his classmates watched. We were all shattered. I still pray for his family.

In my memory, I sometimes get Sept. 11 and the day Geoffrey died confused. The shattered hearts of the communities were similar. In Boston, we were grieving in groups, sharing hugs, tears, and even screams of disbelief and grief. The pain ran deep. There isn't much worse than looking into the eyes of a teenager that just watched their best friend die needlessly in front of them as they ask you "Why?" In practiced fashion, I held the pain back rather than let it out, eventually drinking it away.

One night, I told Edie that I just needed one night of quiet, of peace so I could sleep, to be alone without anyone hanging out to party. We often partied late into the night with folks from the restaurant, frequently hosting them at our place. Edie agreed, or so I thought.

I went to bed and was later awoken by loud voices, laughter, music, and people being generally obnoxious. I was furious with her, with Edie for violating my trust like that. I was so furious that I moved out the next day without explanation or a single word of goodbye. I didn't need that in my life.

But without Edie, I wouldn't have met Jason.

Not long after our falling out, Edie and I reconnected shortly before she moved to Utah, where she'd gotten a job working in the same restaurant as Jason's brother, whom he'd gone to visit at Thanksgiving. When the two met, she told Jason that we'd make a great match and worked to set us up, messaging me repeatedly on Facebook about how I *had* to meet this guy.

Having been married and divorced in the months between graduate school and entering the workforce, I was now living in my own little place, one that even had a parking spot - prime real estate in Boston - and was still near the train station. I loved my job and was doing Zumba and hip-hop classes five days a week with a group of women that collectively dubbed ourselves "The Gangsta Bears." I had zero desire to get involved with anyone.

But then I relented and thought, "Okay, fine. I'll Facebook message him." When our chat conversations revealed his wicked sense of humor, I decided that he was worth meeting. One of the messages still makes me smile. It went something like this:

"Honestly, I'm generally not a random email guy, so I don't know exactly what I should be writing here. I figure there are a few ways to play it:

1. *The 'I don't really understand the point of Facebook' poke*
2. *The boring 'book about me message' - Hi, my name is Jason. I live on the Cape. I am a social worker. I have two sons. I like sports and books. I like to eat food. At night, I sleep.*
3. *The 'be as witty and clever as possible,' which I'm already trying too hard at, so…*
4. *Or this one, 'Edie says you're a cool person. I'm glad you friended me because I was able to do the whole Facebook thing and see a bit about you. You do seem to be an interesting and cool person. If you have an interest in getting together at all, send me a message back and we can set it up."*

He told me he would be in Boston in February, starting graduate school in Cambridge, then asked where he could find that 3-D dodgeball he'd seen on my profile, "Because that may be the greatest thing I've ever seen."

A few days after Christmas, I went to Cape Cod under the guise of meeting up with my friend Peggy, with a plan to return after dinner with Jason. The dinner happened, but anything involving Peggy's did not.

When he opened his door, the first thing I noticed about Jason was his gray sweater. Then his eyes, which are crystal blue and sparkle when he smiles. Then I noticed his smile.

My husband is hilarious. So fucking funny. Razor sharp wit. My cheeks hurt so much from laughing, but it was a kind of pain I could easily endure for the rest of my life. The joy I felt was the best feeling ever. He is the funniest person I know and that will never get old.

The night of our first date, Jason and I went to his house where we sat by the fire and fell asleep. We woke up the next morning in his bed to the sound of a car pulling into the driveway, then children's voices and a knock on the door.

"Shit! Throw this on!" Jason said, tossing me a blanket and ushering me into his bedroom. "Stay in here and don't come out."

I was torn between wanting to see what was happening and realizing I was now shut up in his bedroom the morning after our first date. The entire situation seemed hilarious to me and I tried not to laugh. I surmised that it was his ex-wife and his two sons and peeked out the window to see what she looked like. All I could make out was that she was tall. Really fucking tall compared to me.

As I waited, naked beneath the blanket, for what felt like forever, Jason finally came back into the room.

"Legos," he said.

"Legos," I repeated. "They needed their Legos?"

"Apparently," he said, trying to catch his breath, his face red from embarrassment. We burst out laughing for a good while, then went to breakfast and for a walk on a nearby beach.

I'd ended up having to stay at Jason's house partly because we'd both had so much to drink. There was no way I could drive from his house back to Mashpee, or anywhere else for that matter, and neither was there any chance Jason could get me there. The rest, as they say, is history.

Our relationship moved quickly after that. I remember meeting his kids for the first time, something that must have been so strange for them. At the time, they were 7 and almost 9. Sean, his youngest, was silly and entertained us by crawling on the floor and barking like a dog. We all watched a movie together and Sean was very affectionate, snuggling up with me. He was witty and charming, just like his dad, obviously trying to impress the ladies. Holden, meanwhile, was quiet and super polite. A bit shy and nervous, but so incredibly polite.

A year after meeting, Jason and I were engaged. Though we got along well and were happy, ours was a perfect storm of challenges brought on by our respective pasts. The combination of his perfectionism and fears of anything being out of control combined with my being completely off the rails and continuing to spiral was combustible. It didn't help that he drank a lot with me in those days, and trust me when I say that anyone trying to keep up with me would need to drink A LOT.

For me, it was about numbing a lifetime of pain and dysfunction. For Jason, drinking helped him drop his anxious walls and enter a feeling of freedom. We connected deeply when we were drinking, but when we were sober, or when he was, that level of depth was often absent. It was when I got sober that I realized that this was not a healthy dynamic, and that such feelings should be attainable without alcohol. But I wasn't alone in that dynamic.

All that I'd witnessed in my family, from my mother's drunken bouts with abusive men, to my father's flagrant affair while still married to Maggie, and even her taking him back, had made romantic relationships immensely difficult for me. I was beyond wary of trusting people, though looking back now I see that trust was something I'd never had and therefore wasn't able to fully comprehend. It simply wasn't something I was familiar with.

Loving my mother so much and having her leave my life during important years in my growth was agonizing. What made it worse was that I had no clue how to understand, process, or properly express painful emotions. As I hadn't had healthy behaviors modeled for me, I didn't know what they looked like. Alcohol would make me feel so much better, largely by dulling the pain, so I was able to drop my guard, be more carefree, and talk more freely about myself without the risk of being harmed in some way. When I was sober, I didn't know who I was. The insecurity and anxiety were consuming.

When I lived in Boston, while Jason and I were dating, it was easier to hide the depths of my alcoholism. But once I moved to the Cape, it wasn't so simple. Jason, an intensely private person, was blindsided by the severity of my illness. Loving someone is difficult enough on its own. Loving with an addiction is an immense challenge. So, too, is being an addict and loving someone who isn't, especially when they enable you, hoping that one day you'll get better. There's so much fear. It wriggles its way in and wedges itself between the love, healing, communication, and honesty. On both sides.

Neither one of us was right or wrong in how we handled each other from when we met until I finally got sober. There couldn't be as there isn't a road map for that shit. There is, however, a shared responsibility to strive for further healing once the addicted person gets sober. But that part took time.

I remember him cautioning me not to drink too much on our wedding day and in my head I was like, "Yeah, okay." I was more concerned with nothing awful happening during the celebration. Little did I know that the awful thing would happen because of me.

Everyone at the wedding had been drinking throughout the day, continuing on as the reception lingered into the night. Somewhere around midnight, I realized I was super drunk and wanted to go home. To get out of there. When Jason tried telling me that our ride hadn't come yet, I, in my drunken, annoyed state was so put off by this answer, by not being able to hide in my shame safely at home, took a swing at my new husband, landing an ineffectual punch on his chin as I shouted that I was leaving.

At times, I've questioned why he didn't haul me off to rehab and demand that I get sober immediately, but knowing him as well as I do, I can understand why he didn't. As previously mentioned, my husband is a private person. I'm sure the weight of revealing to the world, particularly the one in which he'd grown up, that he'd married someone in as much trouble as I was had given him more than a little pause.

Because neither of us had genuinely addressed our own issues prior to speaking our vows before friends and family, there was a good deal of arguing during the early years of our marriage. Initially, I thought Jason's anger was at me for being the drunk that I was. It wasn't until later that I understood that he was struggling with his own unresolved resentment regarding situations in his own life. While my drinking was certainly at the forefront of our dysfunction, he, too, had baggage to sort through. Mine just seemed a whole lot heavier.

❧ 14 ❧

IVORY

It was assembly day at Brookline High School where I was employed as a social worker. One of the students in the assembly, the subject of which I can't remember, was being super loud and disruptive, shouting and getting louder despite the efforts of administrators and educators to quiet her down. As the other students laughed harder, the girl grew louder and louder until she was finally asked to leave the auditorium. Her destination? The dean's office.

I watched from across the way, her strength and stamina catching my attention as she stormed out. I smiled when I was called to the dean's office next. I stepped inside and said to the girl, "Come on, Ivory. Let's chat."

She gave me a withering stare and told me she didn't need a counselor as there was nothing wrong with her. I held her gaze and gave her the choice of remaining in the dean's office, which meant getting into trouble, or coming with me and working things out. Ivory decided to come with me.

I loved her fire. Ivory didn't give a flying fuck what anyone else thought about her. It was the first time I'd seen that in another person besides my mother. She was very guarded with me at first, wary of sharing too much, though she did tell me she had numerous siblings that she adored. I mentioned wanting to meet them and offered to do a home visit in the hopes of gaining further insight into this tough-as-nails young woman.

Her living environment was frightening, to say the least. There was laundry - whether clean or dirty I had no idea - everywhere. The toilet was broken and the air bore myriad scents, not all of them pleasant.

I talked with Ivory's mother and the housing department to see what we could do about the apparent chaos of Ivory's home life. I did some of the laundry and held the newborn baby. The Department of Children and Families, DCF, had already been involved and cases involving several of the children were still open. I advocated constantly for the family with DCF, but little action was taken.

And yet, Ivory continued to grow and evolve, becoming a beautiful poet with the biggest laugh I've ever heard. She stuck in my heart and we stuck together. I became another guiding force in her life - a big sister, a mother, whatever it was she needed me to be. I was thrilled when she graduated and even more so when she bloomed following graduation. I saw her often and was looking forward to having her meet Blessing.

Then we lost touch for a while. One day, out of the blue, she called me to tell me she was pregnant. My first thought was, "Oh no! She's so young!" I just wanted her to experience being young without the worries of parenthood, at least for a little while. My second thought was how lucky that baby was to have Ivory as a mother.

She visited more in the months leading up to the birth, embracing her pregnancy. She was radiant, a stunning vision.

One day we were looking up baby names and I suggested Zola, a name that means tranquil, peaceful, and with the Earth. Ivory wasn't sold on the name at first, but had obviously given it more thought because a few months later she called and told me she was in labor. I drove to Boston to meet her daughter, Zola, nicknamed Zo Zo. The world had another little Ivory in it and I couldn't have been prouder.

Ivory taught me that some relationships are meant to be more than how they might initially present themselves in life. It's all about paying attention, really paying attention to energy, spirit, and love, from which we can take what we need. Ivory and I needed each other when we first met. We still do and probably always will.

A strange irony is that I met Ivory the year before my mother died. Sometimes, she'll say things, certain phrases or sayings in nearly the same way my mother did. Each time it makes me smile, knowing our connection is deeper than most people understand.

Ivory celebrates birthdays and anniversaries with us, and there's always cheesecake. Why? Cheesecake was my mother's absolute favorite dessert. I still honor the anniversary of her death and celebrate her birthday with a shit ton of cheesecake, and a whole lot of crass, because why the fuck not? I will do so until the day I die, ideally with Ivory, Zola, Jason, and Blessing, each of whom lights up my world.

15

AN AFFAIR TO REMEMBER

In spite of her behavior, my mother was so powerful in what she said and how she loved me, that even when she looked like a hot mess, I knew there was a formidable woman in there, beyond all the shit. When she was sober and clear headed, she would make sure we had time together and was big on sharing her wisdom.

A feminist, she told me often how women were far smarter than men, and because of this, I had nothing to worry about. She instilled in me some strong values that have made me unshakeable in ways, despite appearances to the contrary.

But it was and remains so difficult to reconcile the strength I saw with the woman she could be far too frequently. She treated her body horribly, wouldn't take the anti-anxiety medication that she'd been prescribed, and smoked at least two packs of cigarettes a day from the time she was 10 years old. Even in the hospital and on oxygen. I'd visit her after yet another roof trip and wonder, "How the fuck do you smell like smoke?" She could charm the pants off of just about anyone.

My father wasn't the only one with commitment issues. My mother had an affair with a married man she met through her work at the TV station in Boston where she was his secretary and on the switchboard. My mom wrote to Peter all the time, whether they were together or not. They had a love affair like no other. She was madly in love with him. I didn't realize how much until after she died, and I found journal upon journal with entries all about him.

She filled page after page with Peter, everything from love letters to poems to painful sob stories of a broken heart. *Peter - Why haven't you called? I have so much to say to you. What are you thinking? Will next weekend be spent saying goodbye? The thought of it twists me. But if you go back, I would like to say goodbye. Whatever will I do without you? I have the strength to be without you, but not the desire, nor the inclination. I would not have the happiness to live without you. My smiles would be empty. If you choose to go back, I will get through it, but I can't ever try again. I will love you no matter what. - June 1980*

Peter was married and had a daughter. That's all I knew about him. He came over a lot when we lived in Cambridge, across from the Charles River. He was there when she was drunk and would often try unsuccessfully to put her to bed. The drunken evenings always ended with her sobbing mournfully about why they couldn't be fully together. I would hear her wailing at the end of the night before begging him to stay.

I remember him being kind. He didn't say much, but his presence was felt. *My birthday. You arrive with a dozen roses. I love you. There is a surprise party with flowers and champagne in the broadcast department. Yani and I spend a quiet evening together. She doesn't understand why there is no celebration. She gave me her present this morning. Tonight we put up Christmas lights and baked cookies. She finally understands why I don't mind no celebration, and that to be with each other is enough. - Dec. 1980*

As I've reviewed my life with her, I've wondered on more than one occasion what her life might have looked like had she truly gotten sober. Where might she have gone? She was the head switchboard secretary at Channel 2, but had the intelligence and savvy to do so much more. But what? In my opinion she had the same energy and intensity, the same promise, as Oprah and could easily have become like that had she not gone the route she had. She was that caliber of person.

Back to the doctor to find out how pregnant I am. I am into the second trimester. You told me you are not ready to be another father. I need you now. I am trapped inside this body. Mt. Auburn Street has become my tomb. I have been buried alive at 205. If it weren't so true, it might be funny. This was supposed to be a happy home. The first one for me in many years. It has become my prison. I don't like to care for it. I don't care about it. I don't care about me. - Jan. 1, 1981

She didn't write after that. She stopped working at WGBH, the only place she felt worthy. She lost her job, she lost Peter, she lost the apartment, and she lost her baby. Then she lost herself completely to the booze, and eventually lost me, too.

❦ 16 ❦

THE REUNION

When I moved to the Cape to be with Jason, I hoped the change would help me eradicate, or at the very least, curb my drinking. Then came my 20-year college reunion, not long after my mother died. Right before I left for Boston, Jason and I got into an argument that set me off. As I drove, far too fast on a highway not meant for high speeds, I drank in my car throughout the hour it took to get from the Cape to Boston. Upon arriving, I was immediately flooded with all the baggage, all of the residual shit that I'd carried regarding my mother, which further fueled my desire to drink.

As if trying to relive our college days, my friends and I embarked on the classic pub crawl. I hadn't eaten anything that day, had already been drinking, and was now doing shots with my friends. At some point, the alcohol, the memories, and the weighty emotions tied to them combined forces in my mind, bringing about what can only be described as a nervous breakdown.

I was crying and screaming, forcing my friends to call an

ambulance. When I say screaming, I mean hysterically and without stopping. Harsh words symbolizing the feelings I'd pushed away for so long poured forth. "I *hate* you! I feel so alone! I'm all alone!" All of the emotions I'd worked to wall off throughout my troubled life had come bursting to the surface.

The hospital had to call Jason to come pick me up. The shame and embarrassment were overwhelming, the drive back to the Cape silent and somber. I remember thinking on the drive home how I shouldn't drink again, but I was so devastated at what happened that I simply drank it away. My college friends treated me with compassion, but also wariness. I think a part of what led to the breakdown was that the four of us weren't all that close. We were friends, but not deeply, which possibly gave me the space in my head to say, "Well, these people don't know me very well, so it won't matter if I just freak out."

There was a time when just thinking about the reunion incident would make me vomit. There was such a stigma attached to it in my mind, to the point where I couldn't address it at all. That it had happened, and that people had witnessed it, was horrifying for me. It didn't help that the people at the hospital were nasty and cold. I certainly didn't treat them kindly, but it doesn't excuse their nastiness to a person in crisis. Meanwhile, I couldn't get home and have another drink fast enough.

My entire life at that point revolved around two things - caregiving and drinking. I only knew how to take care of others, not myself. Be it through my job as a social worker, at home as a new wife, or with my mother in the years before her death, I was always taking care of someone else, but never filling my own cup, except with something to drink to make me numb.

Given the alcohol-soaked society in which I lived - trust me when I tell you there's practically a liquor store on every corner on Cape Cod - it was easy. Everyone around me drank a little too much and a little too often, so I fit right in.

I was in counseling but managed to lie well enough about the drinking that my therapist had no idea how serious the problem had become. Obviously, this meant that I wasn't doing the work in therapy, either. When the day came that my therapist told me we'd done all that we could, instead of telling her the truth, I simply nodded and smiled and left the office for the last time, likely bound for a bar.

Poor Jason had no idea what to do. He supported me in getting help, but in my mindset his words were as muffled as the grownup voices in the old Charlie Brown television specials. "Wah wah wah wah wah." I knew he'd said *something* about getting help, but I just smiled and nodded while making my way to the fridge for another glass of wine.

You would think that the 20-year reunion and subsequent breakdown, not to mention how truly awful it made me feel, would have been the catalyst for me getting help, but it wasn't. Even with all the shame and guilt, or perhaps because of it, I just continued pouring poison down my throat hoping it would ease things, erase them, or at least take the sting away. It did all of that for a while, but then the cycle of self-destruction would kick in. I'd drink to lessen the pain and then feel awful for drinking yet again. Then, awash in negative emotions and self-loathing, I'd drink. Around and around and around it went until my head was just spinning all of the time.

A difficult moment was when Jason went to talk with my brother about my drinking without my knowledge. I felt deeply betrayed by the secrecy, even if I was aware of the immense need for me to get help. I would have been more comfortable had the two of them sat down and talked with me directly. Instead, they engaged in an intense talk, sharing their feelings and fears through tears. Why wasn't I allowed to see such emotion where I was concerned? Why weren't those tears shared with me? Why wasn't I the recipient of that tenderness? I'm sure they kept their meeting private because of my volatile emotional state, but there's still a part of me that wishes they'd included me.

It was soon after the reunion that Jason and I submitted our application to become foster and hopefully adopted parents to our daughter. We'd tried having a child on our own without success, which for me was a blessing in disguise since I know now that not even getting pregnant would have prevented me from drinking. Instead, I'd have been responsible for creating a child with more issues than he or she ever deserved.

For most people, the foster-to-adopt process is an exciting time of hope and change as they await the day when their family will officially expand. For me it was one of the most terrifying decisions I've ever made. It was a frightening time as I reflected upon my own upbringing, my own downfall. Suddenly, I felt tremendously inadequate, utterly unsure about becoming a mother. What kind of parent would I be given the parenting I'd had?

I also knew that I would finally have to get help. Genuine help. It was perfectly acceptable for me to fuck up my own life, but there was no way I could live with ruining the life of a child that had already had a rough start. I decided that if I poured myself into motherhood, everything else would somehow be alright. And yet, my alcoholism was getting progressively worse.

Blessing came into our lives when she was somewhere around 3 years old. Her existence during those three years had been marked with pain and trauma, much like my own childhood had. She'd been removed from her home at the age of 2 and had been in foster care since. Her story broke my heart, and often still does.

Obviously, the adoption process is thorough and involves a shitload of paperwork, as well as evaluations and home visits. People have asked me how I managed to snow the social workers, but it was easy when they'd only come for a half hour to an hour max. I could be sober and "on" for that brief window of time, and they were never the wiser. All I had to do was smile, make eye contact, and answer their questions.

It helped that I was a social worker myself, that Jason worked for child services, and that Blessing was a happy, well-behaved kid. We did not present as a family in crisis and neither was Blessing in any apparent danger. But overshadowing it all was this niggling feeling of, "please pay no attention to the wine bottles behind the curtain, Dorothy."

Even now, three-plus years sober, I'm still stunned that no one picked anything up. Those supposedly highly trained people missed something pretty damn big.

❧ 17 ❧

MY BLESSING

The first time I met my daughter, I spilled water on the floor, which made her laugh. She would tell the story often.

"Remember when you first met me? You spilled water all over the floor?" Then she'd laugh in her little raspy voice.

I was more nervous meeting a three-year-old girl than anyone I'd previously met in my entire life. Her cheeks were the absolute best, round and full and oh-so squeezable. Then there were her big brown eyes and wide smile. That smile, man. I swear that kid could see right through me. She could look into my own eyes and see my bullshit very clearly. I loved it and at the same time it terrified me.

Blessing was the real deal. She was fiery, loud, spunky, wild, silly, smart, and full of heart. She loves everyone she meets, is a hugger, and is genuinely curious about who each person is beyond their appearance. She loves herself so much it's goddamned amazing. If there is one activity she would do for hours on end, it's dance in front of the mirror naked. It's like she can't get enough of her beautiful self. As a mom, I pray that spunk and self-love never go away.

When she went off to kindergarten, I was terribly afraid. Not because of separation issues. At this point in her little life, she was used to that. For me it was more about her entering a system. I was afraid because she was so loud and so energetic and so unapologetically herself that I feared she would be labeled a misbehaved black adopted kid from the foster care system.

In spite of her tumultuous upbringing prior to joining Jason and I, she was incredibly well-adjusted when she first arrived. You'd think she had been with us from the start. When she first came to us, she would ask, "Is this *my* bed? Is this *my* blanket? Is this *my* bathroom?" and the kicker, "Is this *my* house?" Her tone was almost sarcastic in her high-pitched voice, one eyebrow raised cheekily. It made me laugh. She loved making us laugh. She still does. It seems to ground her in a way I've never seen in a child.

As Blessing gets older, she grows more tenacious and is also becoming more independent and flip. Yep. I said it. She is sassy, has an attitude, and isn't afraid to say what's on her mind in a way that suits her. It's like my mother just swooped right into her little body and took over. The two of us are very strong-willed. Both passionately fierce. We won't back down, even from each other. Though she's only approaching 9, I can't help but wonder what life will be like during the teen years.

\

❧ 18 ❧

MY BROTHER, MY FRIEND

When Blessing came into our lives, my brother was one of the first people I brought her to see. I did not visit my father and Maggie, which didn't sit well with them. But since we hadn't been communicating with any success during this time, if ever, I stuck with what was healthiest for me at the time.

Following the visit with my brother, Maggie called me under the guise of having a chat. Instead, she unloaded a barrage of accusations recounting every wrong she felt I'd committed against her, including questioning why she and my father were not involved in the adoption process. There was no awareness in either of them as to why I chose to omit them. Even after we'd attended therapy together, they still didn't have a single clue, both rooted firmly in their victimhood. Ironically, I don't actually remember the first time they met my daughter, which I find telling.

My brother was born when I was 12 and in seventh grade. I remember that I'd been at choir, practicing a solo onstage when the teacher pulled me aside. She handed me a note that said I would soon have a baby brother and that I should go to a friend's house after school, where I was to wait until it was time to meet him.

He was so tiny and round and reminded me of Superman. His superpowers were evident in the tuft of hair on his little head, his deep brown eyes, and his long lashes. Yep, he'd gotten the eyelashes. My dad's. So did my niece. I'm envious of both. I still want eyelashes like that to this day.

I remember thinking that I would do anything to protect him, this fragile being. The thought of him experiencing anything awful in life was horrible. There was another thought, beneath all of that, a question on why no one felt that way about me, but I pushed it away and focused on Ian.

In spite of the heaps of trauma that had taken place before his arrival into this world, I saw Ian as a ray of light. I gladly babysat him when I could. I remember that he wouldn't fall asleep. It was hilarious. I would put him down for a nap and it was as though he had ninja ears. The second I would try to quietly sneak out of the room, he would open his mouth and wail. One creak of the door or the floor and it was all over. I'd end up sitting in his room for hours, singing to him, being with him, loving him.

I remember feeling a sense of relief that I wasn't alone anymore. We had a strong connection from the day he was born that was unspoken, but deeply understood. I had someone I could be myself with. He was my buddy and to this day we're close, our connection still as strong as ever.

Despite the age difference between Ian and I, we enjoyed spending time together. Saturday mornings were our jam. He would wake me up to watch cartoons and we would laugh and giggle for hours. He brought joy into my world and I inhaled it like a kid devours an ice cream cone. I wanted everything for him in his life that I hadn't gotten.

Quite often, I'd make him pinky swear, his little pinky entwined with mine, to always share with me everything and anything - good or bad. And he did. As he grew, I got to hear about friendships, the girls he had crushes on, his heartbreaks, his travel adventures, and all about the woman who became the love of his life, now his wife.

I wondered if he knew about our father's affair, most of which took place while I was in college. I wondered what he thought about the woman with the long blonde hair who wasn't his mother that came to his baseball and basketball games. I also wondered what Maggie thought. Did she seriously believe she was just a friend that conveniently showed up constantly? What did she make of this figure that represented such betrayal for me, yet was the stroke of the ego for my father? There is no way I will ever be okay with what my father did to Maggie and for involving his children. The only thing they genuinely got right, in my opinion, was creating Ian.

But even him being part of my life didn't stop me from feeling overwhelmed and afraid. Shortly after he was born, I ran away from home and spent two nights in a friend's basement. I was feeling used, asked to take on far more responsibility than a kid my age should, so I took off. It was my way of saying "fuck you" to my parents since I didn't have the ability to actually talk about what I was feeling.

I'm not sure what my brother knows about the past, but I think he's aware that his parents, my father and Maggie, have numerous emotional issues. They still treat him very differently than they do me. He had his laundry done until well past college (and possibly still does), and is doted on. They also pay for just about everything he needs or wants, while I've had to fund most of my own way.

In spite of, or perhaps because of, the differences in our parenting, my brother grew up to be the most incredible man. He is well-rounded, thoughtful, antiracist, loving, and whole. He also did a hell of a job choosing his wife, I might add. Brenna is a bright spirit this world needs and together they created the most amazing little being of light that is their daughter, Thea. Her smile lights up my world and is a perfect blend of each of her parents. I'm sure that little girl's energy can move mountains and douse fires.

For the past few years, I've stuck to a fairly regular bedtime routine. I say goodnight to my mom, then Joey, and then Fern. I also acknowledge how grateful I am for Blessing and Thea being part of this world. It is so important to acknowledge the beings in your world that mean the most to you, especially those that have helped you grow. Thea has helped me soften my soul by shining light into the dark parts that were still there when she came along.

I was so horrified by my first time in Detox that I asked no one from my family to visit. Not Jason, not my father or Maggie, no one. I was deeply ashamed, embarrassed, and just mortified. But my brother came anyway. I wasn't ready to see anyone, and must have looked downright horrid. As we sat in uncomfortable white chairs with a monitor by the door keeping an eye on our exchange, I noticed that Ian had tears in his eyes. I knew then that it was hard for him to see his big sister so broken, unsure as to whether she'd be able to put herself back together again.

It's difficult to truly share your feelings when there's a total stranger in the room with you (in this case, the monitor) and the room is roughly the size of a jail cell. It strips away any hopes of tenderness from the conversation. Even so, just having Ian there was enough. He saw me laid as bare as I ever had been and held me in grace despite the harsh realities of my situation.

That moment of compassion, of true brotherly love, changed my ability to move forward. Where I was sorely lacking it prior to his visit, I now felt a spark of faith that I might be all right in the end. When we let people into the dark places we're so afraid of them seeing, light gets in. That light changes everything. That day, Ian lit a torch for me, casting a light that guided me onward and still does, even now, and for which I am always grateful.

19

DEFAULTING ON MORE THAN
A LOAN

The call came out of the blue. I was eight months into fostering the daughter I'd come to adopt, and life had been a blur of caring for her while not necessarily dealing with my alcoholism. Now there was someone on the other end of the line asking where the loan money was. I had no idea what they were talking about. Not a clue. Boy, howdy, did I get one hell of a quick education.

When I was living in Jamaica Plain, my father was sued for non-payment of my student loans, which were in his name with Maggie as the co-signer. Because they were in his name and not mine, and because my name was never attached to the loans, I had no idea they weren't getting paid. I'd been paying the ones in my name, assuming he'd been keeping up his end of the bargain on paying the rest.

He was sued for an astonishing amount of money and because Maggie's name was also on the loan, she got sucked in. Fortunately for her, someone she'd been seeing at the time (during another off-again period in her on-again, off-again relationship with my father), generously gave over a huge chunk of money to make the problem go away. Otherwise, someone would be going to jail, and it damn sure wasn't me.

Along with the lump sum of money Maggie's "friend" had given, my father made an agreement with the lawyers to pay a certain amount toward the loans each month. It was then decided that I'd pay him $100 a month to cover things.

What I didn't know was that in his mind, student loans were part of the government's attempts to control people of color by keeping them poor and oppressed. Considering himself among them, he felt loans were ridiculous and that paying for education was also foolish, even though he was a professor. He was vehemently opposed to capitalism, but then would ask me what I was getting him for his birthday. Needless to say, the loans did not get paid.

I listened as the voice on the other end of the phone told me that my father hadn't made a single payment in years. Many years. I was so confused. When I questioned the monthly payments he was supposed to be making, I was told that not only was he not paying off my student loan, but had done who-knows-what with the money I'd been sending him each month *for eight years.* EIGHT YEARS of non-payment, and he'd swindled me out of nearly $10,000. His *daughter.* I realized that for the loan collection agency to track me down, they must have been looking for my father for quite some time.

When I called Jason, practically screaming the news over the phone, he was livid. Typically the calmer of the three of us, Jason was absolutely furious and was soon on the phone with my father, laying into him as he'd never done before. He explained that my father had done potentially irreparable damage to the family that went far beyond bad credit.

My father, the narcissist he is, denied everything, offering hollow excuses as he tried convincing Jason that it wasn't his fault. My husband, smart and savvy, demanded statements from the loan holder. It turned out that my father had sent a stack of letters to the loan company explaining why he wasn't able to pay them. His excuses ran the gamut from PTSD and depression, to his disdain for capitalism. I'm sure the latter went over big with them. Talk about a victim mindset!

Fed up, I ordered him to start paying *me* $100 a month and took control of the loans on my own. Then I decided that I didn't want his potentially dirty money and started chipping away at them on my own. But what sunk me was the realization that I couldn't trust my father at all, with anything, ever.

I remember that being a big tipping point in my drinking. Here I was, working so hard to be a mother, a wife, and a functioning member of society, and understand my mother being dead, when suddenly I got proof of my father's duplicitousness. His outright lies. Trying to wrap my mind around it all, especially the part where he took money from me each month, was beyond overwhelming.

But this story, this situation and his handling (or lack thereof) of it, describes him to a tee. Not everyone sees him this way, but for me, the story is a perfect summation of the kind of person he is. Even now, should I try broaching the subject, he denies everything except the accusation that my husband and I treated him like a child.

The loan incident called to mind another that happened years earlier, after my mother had died, and shortly after the day I saw my father at a bar with his girlfriend, the woman he'd cheated on Maggie with for years.

I received a call from a cousin on my mother's side informing me about a letter my father had written, asking for information pertaining to my mother. Apparently, he was trying to find a way to scam Social Security by using his connection to her even though they'd been divorced for decades. A past girlfriend had told him that when her husband had died, she'd received money from Social Security. My father thought it would be a good idea to try doing the same, capitalizing on my mother's death.

What he didn't understand was that my mother had received disability funds for her alcoholism. Since she didn't work, she wasn't paying into Social Security, which meant that there was nothing there upon her death. But that certainly didn't stop my father from his scheming ways, or Maggie from standing up for him.

Ironically, my mother had received a small stipend after it was learned that the state hadn't paid out enough. She'd actually given a significant portion of that money to Maggie as thanks for being there for me when my mother wasn't able to. It wasn't a ton of money, but it was significant to her.

To this day, I still have no idea what my father did with all the money that wasn't his.

20

THE IMPACT OF CONDITIONAL PARENTING

The relationship with my father and Maggie continued to worsen after Blessing came into our lives, particularly after Maggie expressed anger at me at allegedly not being involved in my family's life. There was an overabundance of blame aimed directly at me, accusing me of withholding Blessing from them. While I admit to calling, especially after I'd been drinking and was seeking mothering, Maggie seemed to harbor an incredible amount of resentment. She decided that since I wasn't reaching out enough, she and my father weren't going to bother, either.

I told her unequivocally that such behavior was conditional parenting and not at all healthy. How I was able to find that nugget of truth while being fairly pickled on a regular basis was beyond me, but there it was. Parents, I understood, did not put conditions on love for their children. They set boundaries in healthy, helpful ways, but conditions were not born of love. I told Maggie then that we were in an unhealthy dynamic and stepped back, hoping I could finally heal.

Unfortunately, I was still drinking, and was also full of rage. I was so angry with my father and Maggie, for everything. For lying and cheating and scheming and putting all of the blame on me. Fuck that. When it came to parenting, neither my father nor my mother had a clue.

I do appreciate what my father has been through. He was very open about the abuse he felt he endured as a kid, though we really didn't talk much about many things aside from social justice, racism, and equality. It was his primary narrative. It seemed that since he'd never developed his own sense of self, he latched onto people of color, aligning with their struggle through his victim mindset.

Let me tell you, when you're a person of color with a Black mom and a white dad, and your white dad clutches his victimhood as his identity, the narrative gets old fast. Old and obnoxious and confusing and at times dismissive of the genuine issues I was facing in real life.

What sums up my relationship with my father for me is him uninviting me to his funeral. I'd decided at some point that I needed clearer boundaries between us and limited contact for a while. He seized this time to uninvite me to his funeral, even though he wasn't dying. Not even close. I understand now that when someone who is trying to heal sets boundaries for someone else who is a narcissist, the narcissistic ego flips out. It takes on a life of its own and spares nothing in its path.

It wasn't long before the emails and text messages began, dozens upon dozens between 2018 and 2019, each one chastising me for making such a hurtful decision as he continued to claim he was going to die soon. One text read, "I will not attempt any more communication. You clearly do not want me in your life or in Blessing's life. So be it. If nothing has changed when I die, please do not attend my funeral." The others were similar, and always reinforced the alleged fragility of his life, which, I might add, was not at all fragile. Yes, he's 71 years old. No, he wasn't dying. He wasn't even sick.

During the year he was sending me endless messages regarding his impending death, I had a number of friends diagnosed with breast cancer, actively fighting for their lives. I had five other friends die as a result of addiction, including my best friend from rehab, a man named Joe. I, myself, almost died many times during my own life, and still have moments where I need to fight against the demons I know will kill me if I let them.

I get that my father's messages weren't really about me. In truth, he was fearful of dying and not having a connection with his daughter and granddaughter. It was about his fears. If it had been about me and loving me, the messages would have been different.

As a parent, I understand how difficult that role is. As a stepmother, I understand the difficulties of that role, too. As an adoptive mom who weathered the hellstorm of the Massachusetts Department of Children and Families, I understand how hard it is to be a parent. Bear in mind that I am also a person of color and a person in recovery that *has* to stay aware of her addiction in order to prevent a relapse. I get what it takes to be a parent in today's complicated world.

When you're a parent, you no longer come first. Your child takes that place out of sheer instinct. To me, that means gladly walking through whatever fire I must in order to burn away the trauma as many times as is needed so that Blessing doesn't ever have to feel any of it. If we don't take care of ourselves and our traumas and step out of the victim mindset in order to allow our children to thrive and grow as independent souls, then we have done them a grave disservice.

My father did his best to parent me through his trauma. He

still does. I don't hate him, despite what this book might convey. But I am aware that he won't heal in this lifetime. Because of that, I am letting go of the anger, forgiving when I can, while at the same time always protecting myself and my daughter.

There is a memory of my father I treasure, that I try to call up when I'm angry at him again or filled with disappointment at something he's done or said.

We were living in Newton and I was home sick. I was probably 10 or 11 and had such a high fever I was drifting in and out of awareness, shivering, my body aching everywhere. It was one of those times when I just needed to wait it out and let the fever break.

I'd curled up on the floor with my head in my father's lap. For hours, he rubbed my head as he gazed at me lovingly. He didn't say much, just offered his comfort. It's the best and only real memory I have of him bringing me comfort and peace, being a father in the truest sense. In that moment, his love was unconditional. I didn't have to wonder about it since it was plain. Visible. Almost tangible. He's looked at me that way a few times since, but the moments are so fleeting and clogged with such personal trauma that they don't hold up to this memory, this precious moment, though I wish they did.

21

RATTLED TO MY CORE

Trying to adopt Blessing was kicking up a lot of old trauma, worsening my already precarious relationship with alcohol. I would watch her when she was sleeping, holding her tiny hand, marveling at her deep brown color and how small she was.

"Oh my god," I would think, rattled to my core.

That single intimate touch sparked memories and feelings I'd tried so hard to keep at bay, the trauma of it all sending me spiraling until it was all I could see. But I wasn't aware of my downward trajectory because of how deeply enmeshed I was in my addiction. All I knew was that I was angry, crying, and irritable most of the time.

I started drinking with alarming regularity. I would drink in the morning, unable to face the day without alcohol. I would drink at lunch to fortify myself for the day's remainder. I drank at night to unwind. There was an overwhelming dichotomy of doing something I knew I shouldn't be doing and trying to love my daughter at the same time, while also realizing that I didn't have the tools necessary for any of it. The guilt was paralyzing, and the spiral continued for months.

My husband had no idea what to do. He wanted me to be okay, but at the same time knew that he had no control. He knew he was powerless over alcohol, but I didn't. Yet. Our relationship at the time was simply awful. Sometimes his anguish came through as rage, while other times he'd plead with me to get help. And through it all we were trying to adopt this beautiful little girl who had no idea what a shitstorm she'd landed in.

I tried to do yoga as it was the only place I could be in the moment. I'd feel the need to love Blessing with all of the other chaos happening, and with the understanding that her adoption was not a given. She could be taken from us at any moment. Because of that, there were times I'd be afraid to hug her, so fear-filled was I. It would make me physically ill.

I continued to try and move through it all, but the drinking just took over, as it will when left unchecked. Then came that horrible, fateful day.

It was a Friday. I'd done my typical liquid lunch of chardonnay and perhaps a bite or two of something that might have passed for food, but whether I actually ate is a mystery I'll never solve. The wine, however, was clear, crisp, and cool. It was the end of June and the sunshine was beaming into the restaurant hinting at wonder and possibility. I, meanwhile, felt like complete shit. I'd dropped my daughter at preschool and had basically spent the day trying to find the bottom of a glass of wine.

Before I knew it, it was almost 3 p.m. and nearing time to pick Blessing up from preschool. My eyes were glassy and squinted. I stumbled to the ladies' room to try and get the puff out of my face and brush my teeth hoping to hide the wine smell. A glance in the mirror told me my efforts had been for naught as everything about me resembled my mother, including the puffy face and stale booze breath.

At that moment, I hated myself more than anything or anyone in the world. I hated myself for becoming my mother, fully and completely, save for the abusive men, and for being that mother that either didn't or couldn't pick her kid up from school because she was passed out or too drunk to drive.

Teetering on the edge of delving further down the rabbit hole by driving drunk and endangering a whole host of lives, I paused, and for the first time didn't wish everything away as I reached for my phone.

I have no idea what I said, but I fumbled through my story, explaining to my husband, finally, that I needed help. That I'd almost driven drunk with our daughter in the car. The truth was, I'd driven drunk with her in the car before, but not to the level I was at on that day. How I didn't end up in jail I'll never know.

I told my husband it was bad. Really bad. Could he please take me to the hospital and also have someone pick Blessing up from preschool? In a calm, steady voice that grounded me to my very bones, he said, "I'll be right there." It was as if he had been waiting on that phone call his entire life.

The drive was agonizing. Since I knew too many people at the local hospital, Jason took me to Plymouth. In the emergency room, it was as if I was caught in a cyclone. Blood tests were taken, along with my temperature and blood pressure, as well as a visual body scan. I was peppered with a million questions.

"Ma'am, are you suicidal?" The nurse asked.

"What?" I whispered; the bright lights of the ER were blinding. "Can you repeat that please?" My head was pounding, and I desperately wanted more wine. I ached for it. My whole body hurt as if there were tiny needles stuck everywhere along my skin. "I don't want to live, no," I said through my dripping nose and the tears on my face. "It hurts. I need to try to live for my daughter, but I can't figure out how."

The room in the ER, a surreal space of too much sound, too much light, too much everything, suddenly felt like a holding place, a bookmark between my old life and the next chapter. I had the hospital gown on and was sitting on the bed waiting. Waiting for someone to tell me I was okay. That everything I had done up to that moment was forgiven. That this was all just a terrible nightmare.

The walls of that hospital room in Plymouth where I'd begged Jason to take me so we wouldn't run into anyone I knew at Cape Cod Hospital were an off-putting, dismal gray. I was having trouble breathing. When you're a heavy drinker and the alcohol starts to leave your body after months upon months of barely a break, it's a very strange, painful experience. You ache and are so dehydrated. I felt as if my bones were breaking inside my body, and this was just the emergency room. Clearly, I needed to go to detox, but not every facility had a bed open.

As I was lying there in that bleak room, clad in a hospital gown that had seen better days, I saw a window even though there wasn't one anywhere in the room. Suddenly, the room got amazingly bright, but softly, not like the harsh glare of the fluorescents overhead. This was a welcoming, inviting light. I saw the outline of beautiful wings and in that moment felt my mother's presence like never before and missed her more than I thought possible.

Like a child desperate to be held and rocked, I cried, letting the tears stream down my face without bothering to wipe them away. In that moment with my mother, there in that lonely hospital room, I was more present than I had been for more than 20 years.

My first detox experience was nothing short of horrific. The only bed that was open was, ironically, in Jamaica Plain in a dual diagnosis facility. Imagine your worst nightmare of being locked in and multiply that by 100. It was the absolute worst experience of my life.

I really wrestled with that dual diagnosis piece. While I had depression and anxiety, neither was as severe as the mental illnesses I was confronted with in detox. There were people screaming constantly on the ward, people being forcibly restrained. A woman repeatedly tried to climb into my bed and make out with me. I broke up fights between men twice my size since the staff was less than interested in separating them or being overly helpful in any way.

Then there was the Mexican that mooned me.

To be fair, he mooned me and anyone else he could. He called himself "The Mexican" and requested that we all call him the same. He had a Cheshire Cat smile that was a mix of charm and evil. At random moments, he would drop his trousers and show off his ugly butt, sometimes with a slap. That this was my life now was horrifying.

While I understood that profound mental illness was the root cause for such actions, the experience of being put in with these people was nearly as traumatic as the circumstances of my life that had brought on my addiction. I understood the illnesses behind the actions of my fellow clients, but I certainly didn't see myself in the same light.

Then there was the voice of addiction itself, the one that tried, repeatedly, insistently, telling me that I didn't need to be there. That I was fine. Even though the alcohol was slowly, painfully leaving my system, the addiction told me to "get the fuck out of there and get a drink!" It said, "This is not you! You're better than this! You don't have a problem!"

I started to believe that and hated everyone as a result. I

hated my husband for putting me in detox even though it was me who made the call for help. I hated my family for everything I'd been through. My addiction, I decided, was everyone else's fault. Not mine.

When my husband told me he'd found a rehab facility on the Cape, I was torn between a sense of hope that maybe, finally, I'd be rid of this addiction, and telling him to fuck off. When I realized it would be 28 days I said no. Jason had the clinic call me directly and I still said no. I said no for quite some time until I heard that they offered equine therapy and a pool. It was July, so both appealed to me. Finally, after Jason showed me some photos of the place, I relented. "Okay," I said. "I can probably do that."

I opted for the residential treatment program over the day program, but because of the level of shock I was in from the withdrawal of all the alcohol, I was more of a deer in the head-lights than someone ready to heal, utterly overwhelmed by the direction my life was taking. I did some work in rehab, but defi-nitely not enough. I also learned that where 28 days had initially seemed like forever, it isn't nearly long enough for proper heal-ing. It was right around that 28th day that I finally started "get-ting it." Then I was released.

I missed my family terribly and just wanted to go home. Convincing myself that I was fine, I not only opted out of further treatment, but also out of the day program. For the next six months I was sober, and those were the worst six months of my life. Similar to my mother, who had stopped drinking but never healed, I was now a dry drunk. I'd removed the alcohol but not the cause of my addiction. Now my mentality was, "Fuck you for drinking! Why can't I?"

Summer was still in full swing on Cape Cod when I was released from rehab the first time. I was anything but healed and anything but ready. I still had an incredible amount of anger roiling inside me and nowhere to put it. I hadn't bought into the blaming and shaming of AA, and I certainly wasn't going to apologize to my father, but other than that I was empty. I just knew I was furious and needed some way to channel it.

Shortly after I'd returned home, Maggie invited me to come visit with Blessing. As it had only been two weeks and I hadn't really settled in, I told her no. The stress was unimaginable and somehow, I knew I wouldn't be able to stay sober that time around, but I was going to do my best.

Something about my refusal sent my relationship with Maggie spiraling. Maggie took it personally, accusing me of withholding Blessing from her and my father. Maggie's sister contacted me, berating me and telling me that I should consider myself lucky to have two parents that wanted to be involved in my life. Meanwhile, I was doing my best to simply stay afloat and sober and couldn't understand this demand for gratitude when the last thing I felt was thankful. Under duress, I agreed to have lunch with Maggie, which proved a huge mistake. Rather than being supportive, Maggie tried to justify the communication from her sister, but never once heard me.

Further impacting my struggles were the ongoing challenges involved in Blessing's adoption. And yet, somewhere in the midst of all the chaos I'd decided to become a yoga teacher. I was convinced that yoga was going to heal me, and in many ways it did. But because of how fractured our family was, I wasn't happy even though I was technically sober.

This new reality - sullen, moody, bitter wife - didn't jibe with my husband's idea of how it should have gone following rehab. In his mind, becoming sober meant me finally being happy and healthy. If I could just be sober, everything would be fine. Except it wasn't.

I realized that he was sorely mistaken. That there was far more work to be done, and not only by me. It seemed that our issues, personal and those between us, had been magnified by my newfound sobriety. I felt as though nothing was working. I was trying to do good things for myself, but nothing was sticking. I was doing my yoga teacher training and therapy, but didn't feel like I was making any progress. My issues felt amplified, and I was drained from telling my story so many times already.

Other than therapy, the only tool I had to rely on was Alcoholics Anonymous. While this might work wonderfully for many people, it didn't work at all for me. I swore that if I heard one more person in my AA meetings talk about the same damn things they talked about every time, I would go out of my fucking mind. Plus, the AA methodology was completely contradictory to what I was learning in my yoga training. Where AA was all about acknowledging yourself as an addict, or, in my opinion, someone "less than" others who weren't addicts, yoga teacher training focused on stepping into one's power, finding your authentic self, and loving who *you* are. AA basically labeled me as my disease and offered the message that if I didn't go, I was in denial. I simply couldn't buy into this model that was making me feel like a sick person all the time. "Hi, my name is Ayanna and I'm an addict." No. No way. I knew I was so much more than that. SO much more. But AA wanted me to focus first on being an addict, eschewing all else, including the positives. It was the victim mindset on steroids, and I was so done.

The worse I felt, the more people suggested that I wasn't working the program properly. I had a sponsor and went to meetings, and even did my best to follow the 12 Steps, but I struggled mightily with making amends, which is a key principle in the AA model. For example, trying to reconcile the concept of apologizing to a father that had parented me in ways I now find inexcusable for the alcoholism that stemmed directly from that parenting was nearly impossible.

I felt like making amends to myself made much more sense since it was to myself that I did the most damage. I needed to make amends for harming myself, harming my husband, and harming my daughter. What I did do, whether in line with AA or not, was tell Jason, "I take complete responsibility for my actions, and I will take complete responsibility for my healing and my recovery from here on out." I also thanked him for being there during the worst and reminded him that I would eagerly do the same for him. Somehow, I would find my way.

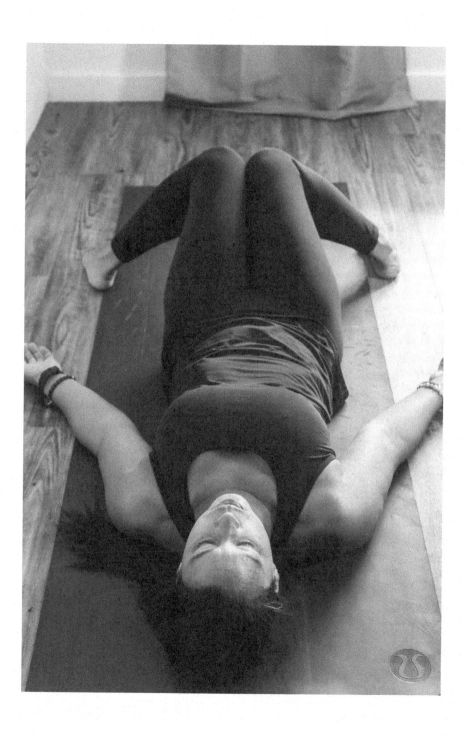

22

MAKING THE ADDICTION
CONNECTION

While my first rehab experience was not the greatest, or that helpful, it did offer insight into the realm of addiction. It became abundantly clear to me that the addiction connection is trauma. There is simply no other way to look at it, in my opinion. Every single person I encountered, either in rehab or AA spoke about a traumatic life event that sent them spiraling out of control. If you're going to treat addiction, you need to treat the trauma. Alcoholics Anonymous doesn't do this. Instead, it seems to take an already hurting person and heap more hurt on them at a time when what they need most is compassion.

Post rehab, I remember walking around feeling, quite literally, like dog shit. Like the gross stuff that sticks to your shoe no matter how much you rub it in the grass. In teacher training, they push you to give up your old stories, all of it, so that you can be present for your teaching. I was fine with that until one session that genuinely floored me.

They wanted us to call up an old childhood memory and

share it with the person next to us. Suddenly, I flashed back to all of those times when my mother hadn't shown up when I'd waited for her train in Newton. Once again, I could feel the anxiousness of scanning the crowd of people stepping from the cars, desperately searching for her face, and the crushing disappointment when she didn't show.

After that class, I was awash in PTSD. I couldn't sleep since all I saw when I closed my eyes were the train tracks and my child self waiting in vain. It seemed there was nothing I could do. I couldn't talk it out, breathe it out, even dance it out. Nothing worked to take me from that fearful place.

It became clear that if I had no other tools and didn't want to die, I needed to drink. So, I contacted my therapist with the intention of telling her I wanted to drink. Except I didn't. I chickened out, then went to a bar, and drank for the first time in six months. Then, because I was so out of control and knew I needed help, I went to an AA meeting. Now, I'm sure as hell not the first person to attend a meeting while drunk, but the thought still makes me laugh, albeit bitterly.

While everyone at the meeting was super nice to me, what were they going to do? Nothing. Dangerously drunk, I got in my car and started driving. On the way to wherever I was going I tried taking a right turn that somehow blew out my tire. Since I knew I shouldn't have been driving, this was actually a blessing since it stopped me and prevented me from going any further.

My husband came and the shit show began. I was screaming, he was screaming and trying to put me in his car, while simultaneously trying to explain to his sons that he needed to take me to the hospital. He was devastated by this turn of events, and very angry.

This time we went straight to the local hospital because of the shape I was in. Once inside, I was screaming at the security guard, quickly becoming "that" alcoholic, the one no one can stand. I berated anyone who crossed my path, from the security personnel to the hospital staff, calling them stupid idiots and whatever other colorful, nasty insults I could conjure up. Years of anger had finally risen to the surface and was being directed at anyone and everyone around me. I was kicking, screaming, calling people names, and yet, was aware enough to know they were not treating me well.

Jason left as security and staff escorted me to a room, still kicking up a mighty fuss. When the staff wouldn't allow me to leave the hospital, I started calling everyone I knew to rescue me, explaining through slurred words and nearly incomprehensible drunk-talk that they needed to come get me since my horrible husband had just dropped me off without reason. In my mind, I sounded perfectly coherent, but in reality I could barely speak.

I called Maggie, sobbing. I called my friend Lisa begging her to come for me. Thank god she didn't. I called Alyssa, the only staffer at my last rehab that I knew would okay this type of call since they came in often.

I had no idea what was going on. As the alcohol slowly drained from my system, the wearing off process set my nerve endings on fire. I felt hollow. At 115 pounds, I was at the lowest weight of my life since high school. Just a week prior, I'd been getting numerous compliments on how great I looked. But rather than bolster my confidence (since there wasn't really anything to bolster by then), it made me feel even worse.

I wasn't strong. There was no muscle tone beneath my skin. I was simply flesh and bone, all sharp edges and hard lines. I had no sense of self, no identity beyond the bottles. Now the bottles were empty, much like me: sharp, painful, dry, empty. I was a vessel full of sand that seemed to collect in my feet, making moving arduous. Everything hurt and I pleaded with the medical team for anything that would make it stop. Finally, they gave me something to ease the pain. Even so, I woke up the next morning still drunk.

Frighteningly, Cape Cod Hospital had no idea what to do with me, so they discharged me without a plan in place. Jason, frustrated and furious, returned to collect me. Because I refused to go to detox, he brought me straight to Recovering Champions, where I'd been before.

The staff that admitted me was skeptical of my ability to get clean. The nurse checked my vital signs and found them off charts. As I hadn't eaten in more than 24 hours, they tried to get me to eat, but it didn't go well and I threw everything back up almost immediately, violently. All I wanted was to go to bed, and they wouldn't allow it.

Instead, they pulled me into a conference room with five other people where they informed me that because of my dangerous vital signs, they had to send me to detox. Still traumatized by my first go-round, I adamantly refused. All I could envision was being mooned by The Mexican or fending off that woman who insisted on trying to get into my bed every night. Unfortunately, the rehab center wouldn't admit me until I'd gone through detox again.

The new place, ironically called "Serenity," was much nicer than the first, and I firmly believe the difference helped me truly begin my healing journey. There were memory foam mattresses on the beds, free massages, and acupuncture. Even the group meetings were different.

When I arrived, I felt like jumping for joy. I felt safe for the first time in my life. I knew I would be taken care of. They had medication to help me with the physically painful aspects of detox and beyond that were so kind to me. Finally, I was being seen.

The stress that I'd been under during the past six months had rendered my appetite almost nonexistent, but when I arrived at Serenity, the first time I ate a meal I wanted to cry. I remember feeling joyful at the realization that food had a place in my body again. That's when the yoga lessons began kicking in.

I'd had to leave teacher training and wasn't even allowed to call and explain why during those first two weeks but I kept up the yoga. I brought out mats and made fellow patients do yoga with me, in detox. It was the most wonderful experience I'd had in my entire life. People were crying from the pain of withdrawal, but they were laughing because I was acting goofy, urging them on by emphasizing, "We can do this!"

It felt empowering, and like I was finally in alignment with my life's purpose. *This* was how to heal. *This* was how to move through trauma, by literally moving my body. *This* was how not to stay attached to addiction. Separation happens through movement in the body. And the breath was also important. I told people, "If you can't move, just lie there and breathe." Then I would tell them to think of positive things. The cool part was seeing them laughing through their tears. The joy they felt, that we all felt just by being around that energy, and in a detox, our bodies broken and our souls bruised, was incredible.

After all, in detox, you're barely alive. If you hadn't gotten there, you'd likely have died. To have people be present in that state, in that awareness, was amazing. It was as if we were all saying, "We did not die!"

I've gotten messages from people telling me that they're alive because I made them do yoga in detox. These are people that have been in detox 25 times. But through those crazy moments on our mats, they saw something that gave them hope. Because of that, because of the new perspective and because they moved their bodies, it helped.

A major catalyst in my healing was being treated with such compassion in detox. It brought me back to being human instead of simply a disease. The shame from addiction is so heavy, so horrible, you feel inhuman. You feel horrid, questioning why anyone would ever want to be around you. When you're in that desperate place and someone puts a kind hand on your back and asks you, in a genuine way, if you're okay, it's powerful.

There is such judgment against people living with addiction. Such stigma. Addicts and alcoholics get used to the faces of disappointment and anger, believing the sentiments behind them to be true. But no one judges themselves more harshly than the addict. That kind hand, that reminder that beneath the illness was a person, was everything for me and set me up for a much different experience when I returned to Recovering Champions for another chance at rehab.

This, the second rehab, was the place where I saw Jason cry, really cry, for the first time. He'd come for a visit with Blessing, his face angry, stoic, like he was a rundown robot.

"What's wrong?" I asked.

"Nothing," he said with a heavy sigh.

I rolled my eyes in annoyance, knowing he wasn't telling me the truth. It was an interaction we had often. He would seem so angry, so unreachable, untouchable, solid brick walls around his heart for days. It hurt my soul. It crushed me every time, leaving me feeling as though I was never enough for him.

I asked again, looking into his eyes. He had tears in them. I had someone take Blessing while I led Jason into a private office. The dam broke and he cried, sobbing, saying over and over again, "I didn't think it would be this hard." He was crying so hard he was shaking, trying to catch his breath, sitting on the floor, trying in vain to wipe the snot from his nose and the tears from his face, embarrassed.

I never loved my husband more than I did at that moment. To me, he looked beautiful. His eyes, though rimmed in red and still leaking tears, were more beautiful than ever. I rubbed his bald head, wiped his tears, and kissed his nose.

"You are a very cute ugly crier," I said. Then I took his face in my hands and, with all the grace I had inside me, whispered, "Thank you."

"For what?" he asked, confused.

"For letting me see you," I told him. "This *is* really hard, but if you can be with me, be real with me, just like this, we can get through it. This is all I need from you, to just be."

After detox, it was on. I was fully immersed in my healing and arrived at rehab with renewed determination. I did yoga every day and understood that the memory of the train was where I needed to start my work. Until I processed that situation and all of the emotions attached to it, I would continue to be stuck, and very likely drunk.

I had a terrific therapist who told me, "I can lead you through this but if it gets too uncomfortable we'll stop." She helped me go back in my mind to that moment. Then she had me visually bring my mother into the picture and hug first the child I once was, and then the woman I became. I recited mantras about how I was safe, that this specific trauma was healed and no longer problematic. It was immensely powerful and shifted everything in my life.

I saw healing visions of my mother apologizing to my little-girl self and my adult self. Because I was able to reframe that image in my mind, to bring healing into it, I am now able to think about the train and not feel like throwing up or shutting down. I'm no longer attached to the trauma. It was this experience that gave me the foundation for my coaching model.

People have the power to shift trauma with their own

thoughts. I believe one place people do that is on their yoga mat. I cried often on my mat, sometimes during group classes, but often on my own. And I had fun, which was something I wasn't familiar with at the time.

The challenge was being in rehab during the holidays, Christmas and New Year's Eve. It meant I wasn't home on Christmas morning when my daughter was opening her gifts. It was excruciatingly painful not waking up with her on Christmas. The guilt of that lingers. I've forgiven myself as much as I can, but there's a piece that's still there. At the time, though, I couldn't focus on that because I knew that if I focused on that, on what I wasn't able to do, it would interfere with my healing, so I did my best to let it go.

In spite of the pain, it turned out to be the best New Year's Eve of my life. I knew I was safe. I was with other people in similar situations and we were all alive. There were people in rehab with me who had been clinically dead and had come back. We were alive and that's what mattered most. That night, as midnight approached, we went outside and danced in the snow, wishing each other a Happy New Year, and I felt hope that it would be.

❧ 23 ❧

SPIRITUAL AWAKENING

In the realm of rehab, there was often talk about some stupid spiritual awakening people had after getting sober. For me, at least the first time around, there was no awakening. Just despair so deep it drove me right into relapse and back into rehab.

The second time around, I came in with a different approach. I tried on different perspectives and tried letting go of what I thought it should feel like to be sober. Each morning we did meditations aimed at helping us calm our minds. In rehab, life is a bit repetitive, almost like "Groundhog Day," which is why what follows is something I'll always remember.

I was sitting there, eyes closed, peaceful. My mind wandered as it usually did. Suddenly, I found my spirit in a graveyard. It was pouring rain, but the rain was warm and comforting. I walked through the graveyard, strangely unfraid. In fact, I felt proud. I was aware that I was searching for something, but not what.

Finally, I found it. There, at my feet, was a small headstone, light gray, with the word "Goodbye" carved into it. A small hole had been dug and in it were the boxes and bottles of wine I drank and hid for so many years - glass bottles of chardonnay piled on top of each other. I started to laugh out loud.

There was a small shovel next to the headstone. I picked it up and began heaping dirt into the hole, over the boxes and bottles, burying those suckers as if my life depended on it. Surprisingly, the soil wasn't heavy. Everything moved with ease and I knew in that moment that was how things should feel if you're moving in the right direction. It might be emotional, but it was also light and free.

I watched as the self in the vision walked away from the headstone as I said goodbye to the alcohol with more ease than I ever thought possible. I took a breath and opened my eyes. I must have had a strange look on my face because everyone was staring at me with worried expressions, asking if I was okay.

"Yes!" I gasped. "Never better!"

I shared with them the vision I'd had, the experience of burying the bottles. I knew it would help someone else. I had to smile when the group leader said, "Welcome to the spiritual awakening of recovery."

After that day, alcohol had no pull over me. The grip it had on me had loosened. I still didn't believe in god, but I had always believed in something greater than myself, and in the human spirit. I knew enough about the Universe then to trust that in that moment, I was right where I needed to be.

❧ 24 ❧

SEEING THE LIGHT

It was then that rehab stuck, and the main reason, the only reason, was that I finally learned to love myself. Find out how to love yourself and the rest will come. But I also chose to attend day treatment this time, knowing that healing is a process. It was so daunting going back into the world, incredibly frightening, but I had a wealth of support. I also had one shining ray of light: Blessing.

A huge part of my motivation to stay sober was my daughter. I understood that part of my addiction was because of what I'd experienced with my own mother, the separation, the abandonment, and I vowed not to do that to Blessing. I couldn't come home the same person I was when I entered rehab. I knew with knife-sharp clarity that if I didn't give my sobriety everything I had, I would be done. I would die, drinking myself into oblivion. I had to break the fucking cycle. At that realization, I would have done anything to heal.

Motherhood is another piece of life's overall puzzle about which I have a different perspective than most on what it entails.

There is no such thing as a good mom. I don't know why people buy into that notion. If she's brutally honest, every mother will tell you it's a struggle. I've even said aloud that I don't always love being a mother. I love my child, but I don't love that I have to be present all the time, to be needed all the time. I don't love that I can't hear my own thoughts. Blessing is beautiful and fierce but her unbridled energy is exhausting.

When you're a parent, you risk losing yourself, your own identity, since you're no longer waking up and making decisions solely for yourself. You are, instead, waking up at the beck and call of someone else, who may or may not be able to function without you for five minutes. If you can't find yourself, find that piece that makes you who you are, it's a scary place to be whether you're an addict or not.

In residential rehab, I didn't have to take care of anyone but myself. Fortunately, rehab taught me that finding a balance between myself and my child is crucial to the well-being of both of us. There has to be harmony, to the best of my abilities, in figuring out how best to take care of myself and match her energy at the same time. If I'm not meeting her energy, we're fighting, caught up in some mother-daughter conflict that isn't healthy for either of us.

Right now, Blessing doesn't know that when I went away, I was in rehab for alcoholism. She thinks, based on the carefully crafted story my husband and I told her, that I was on a yoga retreat. Both times. Eventually, we will tell her the truth, when she's ready. But as we were still immersed in the adoption process, we lied, and no one was the wiser. Since she would have been taken from us immediately had the truth come out, I have no qualms about the lies. I would lie again, knowing that what-ever situation Blessing would have landed in after leaving Jason and me would have been a horrendous nightmare compared to what was happening in our family.

Because I've come to understand, through rehab and the follow-up work I continue to do, the need, the importance of caring for myself, I have helped my daughter to become very independent. She's independent and incredible and creative because I back off, something I admit came from my own mother, though not in the same, unhealthy way. As awful as my mother was in her own addictions, she taught me early on that women are powerful in their own right. That they can become financially stable and that they are their own people. That I am my own being has been an important aspect of my recovery and is perhaps the most important lesson my mother taught me.

25

BURIED TEXT

W hen I decided that my story needed to be told, as well as that of my mother, I reached for the box tucked away in the closet that held each of my mother's journals. There were pages of notes and letters she'd written to me from the streets, written in cars, homeless shelters, tents, and sidewalks. Some were poems and others direct letters to her "Yani Pear." I'd earned the nickname at birth when my face had been shaped like a pear, chubby cheeks and a small head.

While sifting through the box, I found a letter she'd written me in the early 1990s. I'd been in high school. It went something like, "Yani, I need you to know that you are a person of color. You are biracial, but the world will see you as Black. Your father has gone back on his word about this. We agreed on this."

She went on to describe possible scenarios I might encounter, thoughts I might have, people's reactions. I remembered clearly talking about this when I was seven, which made the discovery of the letter that much more profound. Thinking it might make a great lead-in for the book, I snapped a photo of the letter and sent it to my husband. For the following seven months, I forgot about it, only remembering it when I received a text bearing a photo of the letter, allegedly by accident.

I was getting ready to go to an event for my business and was packing cherished items when I saw the text. It was the photo of the letter that I'd thought I'd sent to Jason. Only this text was from Maggie. At this point, our relationship was rocky. She and my father both had a penchant for taking things personally and using their trauma as an excuse to blame our dysfunction on me. I'd seen them last at Thanksgiving and not much since. It was now May.

You might think that a simple text message wouldn't be a big deal, but it was, and what followed impacted my life with such force I was reaching for my rehab tools every stretch of the way in order to manage all that was happening and essentially stay alive.

What is this? I texted back.

It was meant for your father, she replied. *He wanted to see it again.*

She went on to tell me it had nothing to do with her, that it was between my father and I. *This does not involve me,* she wrote.

I called her out.

It certainly does now.

I turned my phone off so I could pause and gather my thoughts, breathing slowly and doing my best to focus on the event and not the text messages. My mind was racing. Did she really have that text for seven months? She'd said absolutely nothing about it. Hadn't responded when it inadvertently arrived in her messages. Hadn't even questioned it. So why now? Why send it to my dad now? Why send it to me? Was it really acci-dental? What game was the Universe playing here?

I didn't reply to her messages but wrestled with my thoughts.

I tried to separate myself from the situation enough to understand my rage regarding her silence when the photo was first sent and the silence that followed. So much silence.

I tried to understand what I would do if my stepson sent me a text like that from his dead mother and what my response would be. It probably would have been me asking, "Are you okay? Did you mean to send this to me?" I would have asked him if he needed something and where he'd found the letter, each question an attempt to make sure he was okay. But my relationship with my stepsons is vastly different from the relationship I have with Maggie. Hers and mine is far more complex. But that complexity didn't change the fact that the original letter had been written to me by my own mother and belonged to me. It was sent to her by accident and instead of saying something then, she chose silence.

Shortly after shutting off the phone, I received an email from my father. Clearly, he and Maggie had communicated about the interaction between her and I about the photo. Instead of calling, he sent an email. A rather lengthy email, once again demonstrating that having an honest, clear conversation face-to-face was not his strong suit.

The email was mostly him defending himself. He went on and on about how my mother's letter was untrue, that she was just trying to sabotage him. I laughed as I read this as he was clearly deeply concerned with his image, worried that this "new" information might be shared publicly. What he failed to understand was that I'd had the conversation about race with my mother many times while she was alive, beginning at age seven. Back then, there was no animosity towards my father, no anger, no confusion. Everything made sense to me. Both of my parents had strong opinions about the matter and rightly so. But the pages of endless defending on my father's part went on and on, interwoven with not-so-subtle blame, not of my mother but of me.

We exchanged emails on the subject for a while, back and forth in a cycle of non-understanding. He accused me of not being able to talk things out, but his words were so cutting in his emails, I couldn't imagine what he'd do to me verbally. For better or worse, I made a different choice.

I called Maggie.

For years, she had been the mediator when needed between my father and I. That ended when the loan situation arose, and she wanted no part of it. She backed down, removed herself, and then unleashed the tiger without a buffer, knowing full well my father's capability for harm, especially towards me. Despite all of her pleas for a closer connection with me, when the shit hit the fan, she chose him.

But I figured that if I could hear her side of things, listen to her point of view, it would somehow lead to understanding. I thought direct communication was the way to go. Boy, was I wrong. Somewhere in between blaming me for not being super nice to her at my brother's wedding, questioning my child's intentions, and feeling insecure about my stepson's opinions of her, I was over it.

"I just want to check in about the text you sent and why you would not tell me you had it, and why you chose to share it with my father without asking or letting me know," I said, then added, "I'm super upset so I am going to try and have this conversation as calmly as I can."

She went on to explain that she was so upset by the letter and the way my mother spoke about my father that she couldn't talk with me about it. "I just wasn't ready," she stated.

Seven months apparently wasn't long enough for her to process a letter she claimed had nothing to do with her but that she was apparently extremely hurt by. "It was about your father. He had a right to see it," she said. No mention of me, of my reaction, my feelings, or any acknowledgement that this was *my* dead mother we were referring to.

I was enraged. She was so extremely hurt by the letter? *She* was? That was not the reaction I'd imagined, and it killed me. It was all about her. If I didn't console her or soothe her feelings about the situation, I was the unsupportive one. I wasn't being nice or understanding or kind. I was so filled with rage I couldn't speak.

Maggie continued with stories of how I've been unkind to her. Of how horrible my behavior was at Thanksgiving. How frightening my behavior was when we met for the first time after my first rehab stay. How she couldn't believe she'd had this person in her home that treated her so poorly on a holiday. Now she was so concerned at how my brother would perceive all of this and whether I would tell him.

Ah. There was the real worry. My dad and Maggie were often worried about my baby brother and protecting him from any harmful perception of them. They were constantly anxious about what I would say, whether I would tell him the truth about certain things. I kept reminding myself that if they didn't want me to share their shortcomings with him and with the world, they should have behaved better. I certainly didn't choose to have my father include me in his affairs with women he wasn't married to.

But Maggie was partly right about my demeanor following rehab. It was a monumental struggle adjusting to life after rehab. I was already challenged by living sober and had added to that my father's betrayal with the loans, not to mention Maggie's lack of parental protectiveness for me, that I just needed to withdraw a little. So, I retreated. I just wanted to spend time with my daughter and husband.

Two weeks after I'd been discharged, Maggie invited me to

the house while some of her relatives were visiting. Knowing it would be overwhelming, I declined. Shortly afterwards, I received a passive-aggressive text from her sister urging me to meet with Maggie for a chat even though I knew it wasn't a wise idea. It didn't go well, and Maggie alleged that she was so scared of me that she'd held her phone close in case she needed to call someone.

I was angry. I spoke in a stern voice, but one that was carefully measured and never raised. Sometimes when strong women assert themselves and hold other people accountable, it can be scary for those being held accountable.

As Maggie recounted her fears during our intense meeting, I had to chuckle. It might have been an intense meeting, but I don't physically harm people. If you touched my child, I can't say I would have restraint, but otherwise, I am a loving person. You can be loving and angry. They can share the same space sometimes. Anger is simply a reaction to how much someone has hurt you, sending your mind and body into protection mode. That's what that was that day we met.

Maggie proceeded to tell me that I must have told Blessing something unpleasant about her and my father because my daughter had asked whether they slept in the same bed. That's a question my daughter asked almost everyone, the question borne out of a life spent sleeping in so many different places that she tries to make sense of the world and the people around her by asking where they sleep. It was merely the question of an innocent child seeking clarity, not making judgments.

Maggie then told me how mean to her I'd been at the hairdressers on the day of my brother's wedding. That I didn't speak to her or meet whatever need I had no idea she needed met that day. My brother's wedding was the first real function I'd been to sober and I was scared shitless. I was sure I was going to fuck it up somehow. That I would drink and make a scene. I could barely keep my wits together enough to relax my jaw for fear of a drink finding its way in. I wasn't mean, but neither was I super bubbly. I was just terrified. For whatever reason, Maggie couldn't understand that.

On and on Maggie went, telling me that I was unkind to her at Brenna's wedding shower, that I didn't pay enough attention to her instead of Blessing, who'd just begun living with us and needed me. I started to see red and knew it was time to get off the phone. I stated that I would share whatever I wanted with my brother as we're both adults even as Maggie begged me not to. She then offered an apology for the letter and the texts, but by then it was too late. The time for that was when she first received the photo.

Before I hung up, she asked if she'd still be having Blessing over on an agreed upon evening. I said no. When she questioned me, I told her my truth. "Right now, I don't trust you emotionally, so why would I trust that you would keep my daughter emotionally safe?"

The emails from my father continued after that, growing worse in their content. He blamed me for feeling angry with Maggie since all she'd ever done was support me. Sure. She did, at times. But to remain silent for seven months and then attempt to create chaos was the most hurtful thing she has done.

I read about how my father was always there for my mother when they were married. My father staunchly defended his honor, reminding me that he was a good person and that what my mother had said in her letter was untrue. He described all of the nights he sat up with her when she was drunk and crying about a dead baby.

Dead baby? My father was not in the business of reflecting upon how what he said or did might impact me, which is why he tossed out the comment about a dead baby so casually. Maybe I knew about it and maybe I didn't. Maybe I didn't want to know. Did it matter? At that point, I was so fragile in my sobriety that everything affected me. It wasn't anyone's fault, but it would have been nice for my father to have some awareness.

I couldn't stop thinking about the dead baby. What was the context? Was it before me or after? My body suddenly felt like an unraveled wet paper towel that just continued to be torn apart. I decided to go to bed and just rest. To try to just be, without so many emotions swirling about.

In the middle of the night, I woke up and headed into the bathroom. As I sat on the toilet, I began to shake. I could see my mom's face soaked with tears. It was the most intense flashback I have ever had.

The baby's name was Rosie. My mother had gotten pregnant by her lover, by Peter, with whom she worked at WGBH in Boston. She lost the baby and was devastated. She loved Peter more than she ever loved herself, which meant that she loved that baby more than anything. After she lost it, she slept and drank and cried for days on end. I would watch over her and make sure she was breathing. I was nine.

I cried on the toilet that night while my body continued to shake violently. I'd had enough. My father was most likely talking about some other miscarriage, but it didn't matter. What mattered was thinking it was okay to tell me about it without any awareness of my emotional state. That it could undo all the work I'd done in rehab never crossed his mind. I cut off all communication with them then. I marvel at the fact that I'm still sober. I am a miracle. To treat me as anything less at this point in my life won't be tolerated. Ain't nobody got time for that.

☙ 26 ❧

THERAPY AND RESOLUTION

After almost a year of limited to no contact with my dad and Maggie, I learned that my brother's wife was about to have a baby. Ian was going to be a dad.

Because of the phone call with Maggie and the emails about a dead baby and neither of them showing any awareness as to how their words and actions might impact me in my tenuous sobriety, I had decided that it was time for me to step back, to protect my well-being. Though difficult, I told them I didn't want contact until I was ready.

If you're a parent, such a request might seem horrifying to you. After all, you're being asked to stop being a part of your child's life. If you aren't narcissistic, you might be able to put your ego aside and understand the need for such space. You might even try to understand what led to that need and extend love and support as a response.

Unfortunately, my father is a classic narcissist, firmly entrenched in the belief that everything is about him, but nothing is his fault. If you need more information on what a narcissist is, try google. I assure you there's no shortage of literature out there.

My father couldn't fathom why I would cut off contact with him. He still doesn't. I tried explaining, but it went nowhere. The more I explained, the more defensive he'd become, mainly in emails, which were harsh, unkind, and filled with blame. Based on those exchanges, I knew that talking wouldn't work either.

He was, in fact, so upset and hurt, he ended up texting me with the demand that I not attend his funeral. I asked him to show his therapist the text that he'd sent to me, his only daughter, the one he allegedly was desperate to have more communication with. I'm sure it was a shock when the therapist agreed with my perception of how cruel such a message was, and that PTSD had certainly distorted his reality. Imagine that.

What I wanted was to find some healing before my brother's baby was born, knowing that once she arrived, the family would spend more time together in order to see her. My hope was to at least come to some understanding, some agreement in which we could interact if not warmly, then as kindly as possible.

We set up a family therapy session in Cambridge with an experienced professional. There is one thing I know for sure about the meetings: if you asked each of us privately what went on in those sessions, each account would be drastically different, especially with regard to intent. I tried to breathe, to listen without judgment, and to ask clarifying questions. Some of that worked and some didn't. I grew frustrated and deeply hurt and wasn't sure how to express my feelings. I felt vulnerable and unprotected.

This is an ideal example of where my own trauma kicks up. I felt unprotected and not cared for by my mother for most of my life. She made the world feel terribly unsafe a good deal of our time together. Most people could probably have sat in that room and not feel instantly like a damaged 8-year-old, but not me. I was already crying on the inside the second I stepped into the elevator that would take us to the floor the therapist's office was on. Already, I was in wounded child mode, each questioning of my actions feeling like slaps to that 8-year-old's face. There seemed to be no shelter from the increasingly frightening storm.

I didn't say much in the few two-hour sessions we had, but a few things did become clear. After multiple questions to my father regarding some of his harmful behaviors toward me, I began to understand that those behaviors were directly related to his trauma. The question then became that, if that was the case, could he interact with me in a way that wasn't hurtful? My father's answer was that he didn't know. As difficult as it was to hear that answer, it was one of the most truthful things I'd heard him say in years in regard to his own emotions and capabilities.

Then the funeral remark came up, along with a few other issues. Maggie stated that from her perspective, she couldn't understand why I gave my father so much power, and questioned why I couldn't just put the hurtful things he said "in a box."

While I understood what she meant, the comment infuriated me. I was so pissed off, I was surprised I stayed in the room. I remain surprised and wonder even now if it was the right decision at the time.

At this point in my life, I have pretty thick skin. I'm able to let most things roll off my back. People have all kinds of opinions of me and I just let them go. As a business owner, you make decisions that people don't like all the time and they let you know that. Not much of it affects me the way it once did.

But then, being newly sober and still struggling to process so many aspects of my life, including being in rehab twice and being a mother, I hadn't quite reached the place where my father could say hurtful things and I'd simply "put them in a box." Instead, my 8-year-old self rose to the forefront as I once again felt the conflicting emotions around the feeling that none of the people tasked with parenting me - my mom, my dad, Maggie - were helpful or supportive.

As an adult, I do have some awareness that them showing up was a symbol of care. I also know that Maggie could have walked away a long time ago and not stuck around when my mother was on the streets doing cocaine and drinking herself into oblivion. As an adult, I understand that her doing so, her willingness to try, was showing love.

But my 8-year-old self has no understanding of any of those things. My mind, heart, and spirit often get confused where my inner child is concerned, especially when it comes to interacting with my dad and Maggie. I continue to work on that, and the little girl within is light years from where she used to be. She continues to grow alongside me and I'm so grateful that I am brave enough to be vulnerable enough to let her.

For me, my wounds got bigger after those meetings, though I was glad I tried. It was an important learning experience and I think if nothing else, they helped each of us gain a clearer sense of where we stood. But even now, I'm still making sense of it all.

During the writing of this book, my dad has had contact with my daughter once a week, usually through phone calls. I, meanwhile, chat with Maggie via text on occasion. She doesn't have contact with Blessing, but we do see her on special occasions, like birthdays and holidays, or at least we did before the pandemic.

It is important that people know this: I love my family immensely. I know there are past traumas at play that make interacting challenging for all of us, especially when they become intertwined. It makes it difficult to separate actual intent from what is said and done. Our relationship is complex, difficult, painful, and hurtful for all of us. It is raw and very real. I meditate on it often.

One thing I know with certainty is that it's critical for me to make sure my emotional health comes first so that I am able to remain sober and be a good wife and mom. I need to make sure I continue to help and heal others by using the gifts that I was given in order to change the world. Through it all, I am aware that who I am is a combination of each member of my family, and for that I am grateful, even for the struggles. In time, our relationships will become what they are supposed to be as we all heal and evolve. I have faith in that. It's that faith that keeps me humble, whole, and keeps me going.

27

EMBARKING ON MY YOGA JOURNEY

As if remaining sober wasn't challenging enough on its own, the process of adopting Blessing was extremely difficult. Between being a foster mom, maintaining my sobriety, and dealing with the broken system that is child services, it was an intensely stressful time. These were the days that I learned about the space in between the triggers, the tears, the breath, the love. I was fully immersed in a chaotic dance of heartbreak and healing.

This is when my yoga journey began. I'd started practicing yoga before I started my recovery journey because I knew that if I couldn't give up alcohol just yet, I needed something to ground me, even in some small way. After all, I was taking an astronomical risk for someone with a past full of landmines, not all of which had detonated.

I had to risk loving this beautiful, whip-smart, sassy kid without knowing whether she would stay with us. It was beyond daunting. I was so afraid to love her, and more afraid to lose her.

She, on the other hand, had no qualms about loving me right

off the bat. It was like BOOM, "There's my mom!" She started calling Jason "dad" within the first week, as well, as if she knew that she'd come home. She fit right in as though she'd been there since her beginning, her big grin and bright eyes just lighting up our whole existence.

And yet, I would build massive walls around my heart that were seemingly impenetrable, so that she couldn't get in just in case the court decided to return her to her biological mother. I wasn't sure I could withstand that level of loss.

The alcohol helped dull the anxiety, at least for me. Blessing, though growing more confident each day, had her own traumas to process, and without the awareness age and experience bring. I would hug her with fear and kiss her with sadness.

The waiting was agonizing and endless. Minutes that felt like hours, and hours like years as we were once again told that the people in charge were doing everything they could despite each court date being pushed back and pushed back again. We waited through visits from social workers that went awry, and when the anxiety bubbled up, I was screaming into the phone almost constantly, pleading with whoever would listen to please have some mercy, some resolve and allow us to finally adopt her.

How we waited for that one call, the one where they'd tell us Blessing was ours. That we were, officially, or should I say, legally, her family. We became a family the moment she walked into our lives.

For me, the waiting felt identical to that of my child self waiting at the train station for my mother to show up. No certainty; just endless hope and heartbreak and crumbling pieces of my spirit.

I did yoga to try and find the space in between where I could preserve myself and allow Blessing to feel love at the same time. Her beautiful, tiny self deserved all the love she could get despite how broken her two mothers were, me and her biological mother. Of that, I was certain.

I would lie on my mat in class and just breathe her in. I would close my eyes and picture her tiny hands and scratchy voice. I would picture her bouncy body that was always in motion and her smile of pure joy. I would keep breathing in her energy as I desperately tried to exhale my fears. I would lie in Supta Baddha Konasana, my knees wide, my left hand over my heart and my right on my belly, just hoping to be vulnerable and safe all in the same space. Fat tears rolled out of the corners of my eyes as I pictured Blessing's big, brown eyes and the way they seem to always sparkle with good mischief, her face a vision of my mother's with its cheeky smirk; I dreamed of all of us living harmoniously, together.

At the time, I thought that was enough. Maybe she could feel my love a bit more that day. Maybe she could see behind my frightened eyes that there were bundles of love and joy just bursting forth for her from that place where there were no walls around my heart. At this point, I knew she loved me more than anyone or anything, and that terrified me most of all.

When we *finally* got the news that we could adopt our sweet girl, I was so relieved. A huge part of me was so fucking grateful, but in the pit of my stomach, the idea of being a mother forever to this boundless wonder was the scariest thing of all. I could still barely take care of myself. My immediate thought was, "Who will I be without my addiction?"

I knew I would have to stay sober. I knew I wouldn't be able to be the best mother to Blessing with Chardonnay leading the way. Nope. When I let everything, all of the clutter, melt away, all I could see was joy, hugs, cuddles, and so much laughter.

❧ 28 ❧

GRADUATION

In spite of all I'd been through, I was able to finally graduate from yoga teacher training. For me, this was a big deal. Huge. It was something I'd stuck with even through rehab, and it was the one thing I was most proud of after getting sober. I was more excited about this graduation than any other.

I'd been trying to foster a stronger relationship with Maggie and my father, making sure to invite them to important events, honoring their wishes to be more involved. I'd send emails with specific details, reminders, and dates. I decided to invite them to my final yoga class and my graduation, which would happen on different dates. Everyone - Maggie, my dad, Ian, and Brenna - came to my final class, which turned out to be great fun. But not everyone came to graduation.

Ivory came, as did Jason's mom, who brought me flowers. Maggie and my dad didn't show. I would have been okay with this had it not been for the phone call I received prior to the ceremony, and what I learned later.

"Yani, we were just on the Cape and I think it would be too much for us to drive down again," Maggie told me. "Is that okay with you?"

I didn't know what to say, so I just said, "I guess." I was extremely confused given that she'd just begged and pleaded to be a bigger part of my life. Now an hour-and-a-half drive was too much?

Although Maggie isn't on Facebook, other friends and family members of hers are, including a sister who seems to funnel a good deal of information to her. After photos were seen online of my graduation celebration, I got a text from Maggie. *We didn't realize it was a graduation and something so important. Otherwise, we would have been there. We had no idea.*

I knew otherwise, but just to be sure, just for shits and giggles, I looked back at the emails I'd sent to make sure I didn't miss sending the graduation invitation to both of them. It was *clearly* there, and there was no mistaking that it was an important milestone for me.

I still tried hanging in there with them after that, inviting them down for a visit later in the summer. At some point during the outing, it was mentioned that Maggie's sister had built a new treehouse at her home in Rochester, New York, roughly eight hours from where my dad and Maggie live. Apparently, the treehouse was so cool, they drove up to see it. Eight hours.

I had a tough time wrapping my mind around that, and couldn't shake the feeling within, almost like being stung. I couldn't understand how it was somehow okay to drive almost an entire day to see a treehouse, but a little more than an hour for my graduation from yoga teacher training was too much. I tried, but it really put a dent in my relationship with my dad and Maggie. I paved the way for them, and they still couldn't show up. It definitely didn't help me feel loved.

But I had that diploma and a new life on the horizon, one of my creation.

29

ADOPTION DAY AND BECOMING A FLAMILY

We became Blessing's Flamily. Yes, you read that right. No, it's not a typo. The most precious thing I heard my daughter say was "flamily." She couldn't say "family" for the longest time, and I loved it. I adored the uniqueness of it. That it was her own word for us. At dinner, she liked to do "cheers" before we ate.

"To what?" Jason and I would say.

"FLAMILY!" Blessing would gleefully reply. Every time. To me, it was the best word ever. I loved the sound of it.

With an official date locked in, Jason and I decided to make a celebration of Blessing's Adoption Day. I was counting on lots of photos, and there had to be cake. Adoption Day, the day on which a child's adoption becomes finalized by the state, is traditionally a big deal. A really Big Deal, often with family members packing the courtroom to witness the moment foster care ends and flamily forever begins.

Jason's parents had booked Jason and I a hotel room in Boston months prior, right near the courthouse, so that we could be right on time for our hearing. We were also throwing an adoption party the following week that was bigger than my wedding reception.

I wrote to my father, Maggie and Ian about Adoption Day, hoping they would attend. My father emailed me and told me he couldn't make it to court, refusing the already tenuous invitation I'd extended.

I decided to share my thoughts regarding his decision not to attend the finalization hearing in a reply-all email. He called, offering a flimsy excuse that he didn't think being at the courthouse would be such a big deal, and added that he was going to come to lunch afterwards, and to the big party, but that he had to teach.

I thought about what my mother would have told him in that moment, the one in which he tried defending his decision to once again drop the parenting ball even though I'd set him up to make a perfect shot. I knew she'd have been beyond pissed, likely calling my father some choice names.

Since she wasn't there and I was, I explained to him quite impatiently what a big deal adoption day is. I emphasized the significance and told him how everyone would cheer at the end, and what a truly important moment it was.

He didn't think it was a big deal, "the hearing part."

I was furious and deeply hurt, to the point where it didn't matter that he ended up being there, lying about how he'd intended to come all along. What mattered most was that my father had initially declined my invitation to such a momentous occasion in my life, in Jason's life, and especially in Blessing's. When I think about how it would impact her, it's unthinkable.

Meanwhile, Jason, I, Blessing, Jason's parents and sons, Blessing's brothers, arrived in Boston the night before Adoption Day, enjoying a celebratory dinner during which we held a last toast as a foster flamily. Then it was time to try and get some sleep on what would be our last night as a temporary team. In the morning, we'd head to court and enter into forever, together.

Though each of us was nearly bursting with excitement, we somehow managed to sleep. The next morning, we got dressed up, so ready for the day that we'd been waiting for, not entirely patiently, for three long years. I was so excited I could barely sit still, the smile on my face stretching its entirety.

The courthouse was awash in finery, gold and shiny. There were little boys wearing bow ties and little girls with flowers, each eager for their own special moment of making a family. The energy inside the courtroom was electric with joy, anticipation, hope, and peace. It is a day that social workers look forward to, especially those that worked diligently each day, doing their best not to take to heart the painful stories behind each adoption. Along with them, the new families were smiling bigger than I had ever seen, the elation palpable.

I noticed two Black boys about four years old, twins who were dressed to the nines. They were becoming a forever family with a lesbian couple that loved them to the ends of the earth. The sight of this family and the love so evident between them brought tears to my eyes, and they were just one of several families making a promise of forever that day.

Another family of about 10 was adopting a single child and each family member wore a custom-made t-shirt that said the child's name and "#forever" on it. There were teenagers unabashedly holding the hands of their new parents as they walked out after being declared family by the presiding judge.

All I could think was, "Thank you. Thank you for this moment, for this day, for all these children finding a home."

They allowed our whole family into the courtroom together, which was amazing to me. We all cried, our emotions on high.

Officials asked if either of the parents wanted to speak. I had Jason speak on my behalf because I was crying too hard to get the words out. He thanked our social worker and then our families, including my mother in his recognition. I cried as they spoke Blessing's "new" name aloud for the first time: Blessing Lake Parrent. Her first name, our last name, and my mother's name right in the middle. That made it real for me, even more than signing the paperwork that allowed us to enter the proceedings, which says a lot since that signature felt like the most important time I'd ever written my name.

So many people dearest to us were there - Ivory and Zola, my brother, Jason's parents. Aside from giving birth, I can't imagine a more significant and powerful moment in my life.

While in the courtroom, through the tears that continued to slip down my cheeks, I wanted to thank Blessing's birth mother. I wanted to thank her for bringing such a beautiful being into this world. I wanted to thank her for doing whatever it was she did to help Blessing become so resilient and joyful, loving and silly. I wanted to tell her that I understood what it was like to struggle, and that I hoped now she might feel a sense of relief knowing that Jason and I were going to love her daughter more than seemed possible. I also took a deep breath and forgave her for anything I was still holding onto, sending her love and gratitude instead. I imagined her sitting with us, allowing the transition, us sharing a silent, special moment as mothers. I wasn't able to verbally express any of these thoughts, but I held space for each one and am sure she heard them.

Then it was Blessing's turn to bang down the wooden gavel, making her adoption official. We were legally, truly, lovingly her flamily. That so many people had shared in our celebration made the moment even sweeter and almost erased my father's ignorance. Almost.

Even after I saw that my father had come to the hearing, I again pondered his almost automatic refusal to be part of this, the actual moment Blessing would legally be our daughter and we her forever family. How could he not understand the significance of the occasion? It hurt doubly since it felt as though he was including Blessing in his decision not to come. That was the part I couldn't allow. It was one thing to blow off his daughter, but mine? Oh hell no. Fuck that.

For some reason, the entire situation reminded me of the time Maggie and my father came to visit us on the Cape, and Maggie completely shut down because she was jealous of Jason's parents. She stopped talking abruptly and became visibly upset. Though my father kept asking her what was wrong, she wouldn't tell him. Then the manipulation started.

At one point, Maggie asked my father to read Blessing a book. His response was, "Not until you tell me what's wrong."

My father wouldn't read my kid a book because he *had* to know what Maggie was upset about? For real? Even I knew the best thing he could have done was to take a step back and read the book. Their dynamic was so tangled.

I asked her about it later and she told me she thought the get-together would be just her, my father, Jason, Blessing, and I. She was jealous of Jason's parents and how close they are with me and with Blessing. I tried to understand that, to understand her meltdown, but I couldn't wrap my head around the fact that she'd chosen to become emotional instead of just engaging with my daughter and I while she had the time to do so.

As if coming to the courthouse had been enough, my father didn't show up to the adoption party. He called that morning and told us his back was out, something that happened enough times to have potential, which was why he was hoping I wouldn't see the lie. Either way, it was possible.

But my gut told me it was something else. That he was emotionally incapable of being there. I knew damn well that if it was me in that position, even if I was in excruciating pain, come hell or high water, I would have made it there on a fucking stretcher carried by handsome EMTs. After all, this celebration was three years in the making. Three years of anxiety and adjustment and healing and hope, and some damn hard work.

Nothing would stop me from being there. Being there is how you show your love, especially to your children, who deserve nothing less. You show up when it matters the most, despite what pain you might be in yourself.

I told Jason that it didn't matter how much pain I was in. If my daughter needed me, I would be there.

I saw my father a week later on Thanksgiving and he was fine, which he definitely wouldn't have been had he not potentially been faking it. I watched him step out of his car and walk up to Maggie's door, coffee cup in hand, as if he'd never had a pain in his life. He made no mention of the party as he passed me by. It was as if I was invisible. But then again, so was he. I'd realized that in order to be brave about the parts of life that hurt beyond measure, we need to see ourselves first, for it is in seeing our own needs, our own fears, our own humanness that we are able to see someone else as they are and not necessarily what we hope them to be.

In spite of the drama, adoption day turned out to be incredibly special. While we were in court, the judge presiding over the adoption brought us back into his chambers. I was holding my breath, panicking inwardly as I expected the worst. Instead, he wanted to tell us that he'd known Blessing from the time she'd been removed from her home by child services at the age of two and was thrilled to be overseeing her adoption.

I was speechless at such a powerful connection. That he'd

known her since the beginning of her foster-to-adoption journey was huge. I was elated that he'd been the one to declare everything official.

After that it was all about the celebration, which was a much bigger celebration than our wedding reception. We'd gone all out, partly because I wanted Blessing never to forget how much she was wanted, how her being in our family was celebrated. I wanted any memories of her adoption to be filled with dancing, bellies full of good food, laughing children everywhere, new and old friends, endless joy, and a new forever family love.

✾ 30 ✾

THE SYSTEM IS BROKEN

Systemic racism is a very frightening thing. Raising a dark-skinned, loud, outspoken child is wonderful, and also terrifying, especially in today's society. As of the writing of this book, we are currently in the midst of the coronavirus pandemic, and another pandemic that's even more insidious: the ongoing scourge of police brutality and white supremacy.

Nationally, we've watched unfold scenes of riots and protests almost nightly on myriad news broadcasts. Locally, even in a small place like Cape Cod, someone has been putting up stickers with the address of a well-known white supremacy website on them.

The difference between the civil unrest now and the Civil Rights Movement of the 1960s is technology. Now we have state-of-the-art phones with cameras that capture each moment in stunning detail. People can record the violence they witness, such as that of Philando Castile, George Floyd, Breonna Taylor, Ahmaud Arbery, Jacob Blake... The list goes on and on. Understandably, Black people are outraged, but so, too, are white people. I'm not sure how I feel about that since so many seem to think the violence is new. It's definitely not.

People of color - Black, Indian, Native American, Hispanic, Asian, Middle Eastern - have been dealing with discrimination and violence for more than 400 years, but it seems to be coming to a head in ugly fashion in 2020. It's a time riddled with conflict. The mainstream news media has every viewer by the balls to the point where no one knows what's truth anymore. Racism certainly existed before Donald Trump was elected, but under his governance it has bloomed into a most poisonous flower.

It is because of this that I have been afraid to send my daughter to school. Public schools are systems run by politics, money, and other, larger, and often more corrupt systems. While individual members of these systems might not be racist, the system as a whole has a deeply racist history that seems predicated on the unspoken rule that if you're born in America, you're born into a country of racist ideals and values that have been woven into the images, concepts, and teachings of American education.

Don't believe me? Ask your child what they know of the first Thanksgiving. Ask them how many books they've read by Black authors. Ask them what the history books have to say about slavery and the Civil Rights Movement. In so many cases, everything has been whitewashed. Thanksgiving is portrayed as a celebration between white settlers and indigenous peoples. *To Kill a Mockingbird* is an incredible book, but Harper Lee was still white. The grim details, the truths about slavery and about the Civil Rights Movement, are often barely a footnote in books that trumpet the successful colonization of America by white men, glossing over the fact that they stole the land from those already here. It is past time to change course from "I don't see color" and "all lives matter."

When the school psychologist called me about halfway through the school year inquiring about Blessing, I wasn't surprised. She's quite a handful. But I will tell you this: as a social worker that dealt primarily with children for many years, I'd seen firsthand what Attention Deficit Disorder, and Attention Deficit Hyperactivity Disorder truly look like. My child had neither ADD, nor ADHD. Was she anxious? Absolutely. Who wouldn't be with a similar start in life? Did she possess a shit-ton of energy that simply couldn't be contained? Hell yes.

It was clear that the school was having difficulty managing all that. The phone call I received in regards was not the most uplifting and ended in an abrupt hang up, by me. Soon after-wards, a paper was sent home by the school psychologist requesting more information about Blessing, with information attached stating that the psychologist had watched her in class and wanted to deepen her observations.

I told the school they had absolutely no permission to do anything of the sort. No observations, no ferreting out informa-tion, nothing. They had been given all of the information I felt was necessary for Blessing to succeed in school. The psychologist called me again upon receiving my note.

"Why don't you want me to speak with her therapist?" She asked. "Isn't she adopted? Wouldn't it be helpful?"

I was ready to kick this woman in the ass. First, Blessing didn't have a therapist as she wasn't in a place where it was necessary. I asked the woman pointedly what her aim was.

"Are you assuming that she's struggling because she's adopted? Or do you think there's some underlying reason she's got so much energy?" I hoped I wasn't shouting.

I informed them that Blessing was very well-adjusted despite all she'd been through. The psychologist, meanwhile, went on to explain what the student support team was, as if I hadn't a clue.

"If they read the information I gave them, the school would know that I was a social worker myself and worked in schools for years," I told her. "Of course I know what the SST is."

She then alluded to Blessing having ADHD, describing each characteristic without actually using the term, possibly hoping I'd trip up and agree with her.

"Let me stop you right there," I told her. "You can stop trying to label my child. You're venturing down a path you shouldn't. You have no evidence of anything other than that she has a lot of energy. You need to get creative around it. STOP trying to diagnose my Black child with something she doesn't have."

I was damn near shaking with fury. While sorry that the teacher had to implement strategies to harness Blessing's energy, I also knew that was her job.

"Blessing has the capability to focus, but like many kids she chooses not to at times. Give her some stickers, some movement breaks, and a lot of attention and she will be just fine," I said. "Goodbye!"

And with that, I hung up.

Like so many that had come before her in our fractured educational system, my daughter was "othered" because of her boisterousness and her skin color, though proving the latter would be difficult in a she-said-she-said scenario. But it reinforced for me that raising Black children is scary. I feel for moms raising Black children, especially Black boys and young men. It is not by chance that Black men are the highest population in jails across the nation. Sometimes, all I can do is just breathe.

Ahmaud Arbery was killed by white men simply for the "crime" of running while being Black. Not running away from anything, except his attackers. Just running for fitness, which he loved to do. In his honor, me, my husband, and Blessing participated in a 5K that took place on what would have been his birthday. As we were getting ready to go, Blessing asked me if she should wear white.

"You can wear whatever you want," I told her.

She looked at me in confusion and pointed to her dark skin. "Shouldn't I wear white just in case those men try to get me when we are running because I have Black skin?"

Fuck.

These were the words that, as a mother, I hoped never to hear. The ones in which my daughter, my beautiful Black daughter, questioned her safety in the wider world.

Jason, I, and Blessing talked a lot about race that day. About protecting yourself, using your voice, about what racism looked like and sounded like, and about the importance of loving yourself in spite of the images you might see that inspire fear. We talked about white people, about her dad, her brothers, her grandparents, and about history and the police.

I can only imagine what a similar conversation must be like between parents and their Black sons.

"I promise to protect you from harm whenever I am with you, but I need you to do something for me," I told her. "Can you promise to let me know if things happen to you when I'm not there? I will promise to listen and help in the best way I can."

"I can do that Mom," she said. We hugged. I cried. I cried a lot that day, not just for Blessing but for Ahmaud's mother and all the mothers that have lost children to police brutality and racism. And then I prayed for it to end.

31

A SIGN OF SUPPORT

As racial tensions around the country rose following the death of George Floyd, Black Lives Matter signs were popping up everywhere, including on Cape Cod. We had one in our yard that lasted a total of 48 hours before someone stole it. While I was deeply frustrated by the theft, my response wasn't one of anger. It was, instead, one of sadness for the person that took it. I can't imagine the ugliness inside of someone that one must feel in order to do something like that. I feel awful for them as it's a sad and lonely place to live.

After the sign was stolen, Jason, Blessing and I went for a long walk together, trying to get off our phones, reconnect with nature, and just be together, knowing that we *do* matter. That our little multi-racial family matters. We matter to each other, first and foremost, and that's more important than any stolen sign.

As we approached our house following the walk, we noticed a new sign. Someone had delivered and erected a new BLM sign on our lawn, filled with color and hearts. There was no note, but the gesture spoke volumes. "You are loved," it told us. "You matter." It was an absolutely amazing gift.

Later that evening, Blessing was hyper and anxious, and couldn't stop talking about god-knows-what, chattering away. I'd encouraged her to get active and get some of that energy out, but it wasn't working. Finally, I took her in my arms and said, "Stop. What is going on, my love?"

Her body shook with fear. She burst into tears, sobbing and saying she was worried that the person that took our sign would come back and hurt us next time. It was a legit fear. She was right to be afraid of something like that. With all that's going on in our nation, it was definitely something to be fearful of.

I held my daughter tight, doing my best to reassure her. I didn't know if anyone would be coming back, but I didn't think so. Either way, Blessing calmed down. Sometimes just witnessing the fear without words is exactly what is needed. I wonder what the sign thief would think if he or she knew the terror they'd instilled in an elementary-school-aged little girl. While I'd hope it might be sadness, my instinct told me they likely wouldn't care.

As the days went on, we received even more gifts. A favorite was a security camera that helped Blessing feel much safer. Our gratitude for these gifts, and for the support shown to us by our community, is immeasurable. It feels like people are finally listening to what we have to say.

32

FERN

Like many school systems across the world, when COVID-19 hit our shores, schools shifted to remote learning. At some point during the surreal days, my daughter proclaimed, "I don't like reading!" Yikes. First, I knew that wasn't true. Second, she was about to get the lecture I'd gotten on the same subject over and over again, but rightly so.

It was a privilege for Black people to read. Saying you didn't want to or didn't like it wasn't an excuse and wasn't allowed when I was growing up, and wouldn't be allowed for my daughter, also.

I sat down and talked with Blessing about slavery, about Harriet Tubman and Frederick Douglass and all of the ancestors that had come before us, paving the way for the opportunities we have today. I told her how the slaves that had been taken from their homeland and brought to our country were forbidden to read, unless it was the Bible.

"Was Martin allowed to read?" She asked, referring to

Martin Luther King, Jr. They do a good job teaching about him in schools, but not many others.

Blessing's next comment floored me.

"Dad says that a long time ago you wouldn't be together because they didn't allow Black and white people to get married," she said.

"That's true, my love. But just like how I found my way to you, I would have found a way to your dad, too," I reassured her.

It was impossible to contemplate race relations without thinking of the powerful women in my family: my cousin Fern, who died in August of 2020, and my great-grandmother, Nanny.

Fern Cunningham was an artist, a sculptor, an activist, and one of my most favorite people on this planet. She was so close to my mother that the first thought I had upon learning of her death was that they finally got to be together, happy and healthy.

My mother and Fern had the same smile. We all did in the Barnes family, wide and, for many of us, me included, with a small gap between our front teeth. In photos you can always tell the Barnes women, including my great-grandmother, Nanny.

Nanny was someone my mother talked of constantly. Nanny this and Nanny that. "Nanny would say..." was a common way to start a sentence. The Barnes women - Nanny, my mother, Fern - were and still are incredible. Black artists, creators, educators, musicians, and much more. Fern was an artist that told stories with her hands, stories of our ancestors, her works representing the African American culture in all its glory.

One of her most famous sculptures was "Step On Board," and is the first sculpture honoring a woman to appear on city-owned land in Boston's South End. The sculpture depicts young Harriet Tubman, Bible in hand, leading men and women to freedom via the Underground Railroad. Another sculpture, of an

African wise woman, called "The Sentinel," stands in Forest Hills Cemetery where Fern was buried.

I had the privilege of attending her funeral, which was small due to the pandemic. Even though she was family, I was blessed to be there. A professor spoke about her work. He said she was interviewed about "Step On Board" and was asked two questions - Why was Harriet Tubman so young and where was her gun? Most representations of Tubman feature an older woman, typically with a gun in her hand. Fern's reply was simple: Tubman was in her glory when she was in her 30s. The Bible was her power, not her gun.

As the professor continued, tears rolled down my face and into my mask, worn as protection from the global pandemic. I pictured Fern's hands moving with grace and purpose as she carefully sculpted Tubman's power. I closed my eyes and envisioned Harriet and Fern meeting in spirit, the scene bringing me comfort. I was, at that moment, incredibly grateful for both of these powerful women.

I brought Blessing to see the sculptures. As she gazed up in awe, I said, "This is why it's a privilege for us to read. We just say 'thank you' and never take it for granted."

Fern has four beautiful children that are all unique in their own right. But one thing we can all agree on is that Fern was a mother to all of us, including her students at the Park School, her children's friends, her cousins, her artist friends, her best friend. We were all so important to her and she had this amazing way of showing it that made you feel like you were always remembered.

It's not uncommon in life to feel lost, especially when our mother dies. My first thought when my mother passed, besides relief for the end of the suffering, was how there was this chasm within me, this space of not knowing how to live in a world when the person that brought you into it isn't there anymore.

Watching Fern's body be interred into the ground near "The Sentinel" was beautiful and heartbreaking. Grief shifts people. It changes them and sometimes stops them in their tracks for a while until they can move through the excruciating pain of immense loss.

As we were leaving the cemetery, Fern's oldest son was standing there, just frozen in place. Images of the two of us playing together as children darted through my mind. He and I were born three days apart. There are these fantastic pictures of when my mom and Fern were pregnant at the same time. Cumaci's heart was ice. He had been through much in his life, as I had, and this was a lot, too. I watched him stare into her grave as they tried shoveling dirt atop the casket but couldn't while he was standing there.

But the Barnes women were there for him. Myself and my cousins Karen, Mikki, and Lisa, we all tried wrapping our hope around him to give him the ability to move. We told him, "She's in your heart. She is in you always. Her spirit is alive and well and she wants you to be okay." As Cumaci stood, Jason tried his best to keep security at bay for as long as possible. I took Cumaci's hand and reminded him of our bond. I told him to look into my eyes.

"Do you trust me?" I asked, quietly.

He nodded; his eyes filled with uncertainty.

"Good," I said. "Because my mom and Fern need us to move and let them be. We can do hard things. Do you trust me?"

He was silent, gazing back at the gaping hole in the ground now bearing his mother's coffin.

"You haven't seen me in a while, Cumaci," I said. "I have big biceps now and can fuckin' muscle you out of here if I need to." I smiled.

He laughed, then. His body moved and he smiled his mother's big smile. I took a breath and told him I loved him bigger than I could show him in that moment. It took a little while longer for him to walk away, but with each of us enfolding him in love, he was eventually able to.

In the days following her funeral, Boston Mayor Marty Walsh declared Aug. 20 as Fern Cunningham day in the city. Fern changed this world more than she will ever know. Her legacy lives on in all of us.

❦ 33 ❧

BREATHE

In the many minutes that have passed since George Floyd was killed, we've seen the signs on the television, social media, and even in our neighborhood protests: I CAN'T BREATHE. But what do they really mean?

For Floyd, it meant a last plea for help as the breath of his life was snuffed out. For protestors, it is yet another plea for law enforcement to please check their racism at the door and be aware of the potential outcome of their actions. It all comes back to the breath.

Breath is everything. It is what tells the world we're alive when we first burst into it from our mother's womb. It is how we steady ourselves in times of unrest. Everything starts with breath - life, healing, making important decisions, taking a step toward a better life. It all begins with breath. Until someone tries to stop it.

I was at a protest in the town of Orleans last spring in which hundreds of those in attendance attempted to kneel for the eight minutes that George Floyd was under the knee of the police officer that ultimately murdered him. I consider myself fit and athletic, and kneeling for that long was a struggle for me. I was painfully uncomfortable, for many reasons. It was astounding to me how difficult it was to simply kneel on the grass, damp and punctuated with pebbles in places. It hurt, and I wasn't anywhere near the level of violence it took to kneel on a man's neck as he struggled to breathe.

George's face kept flashing through my mind, along with that of his daughter. His voice, fear-filled and fading, echoed in my ears as he cried out for his mama. Nearby, I saw an older man of about 70 struggling with the gesture. He really wanted to kneel, for George and for all of us, and he tried his damndest. Ultimately, he fell to the ground and burst into tears, his hands out and his knees on the ground.

I put my hand gently on his back as he cried, and suddenly sensed a current running through the crowd of many races: collective suffering. Earlier that week I'd done a Facebook Live event with one of my favorite yogis, Michelle C. Johnson, who is the author of "Skill in Action: Yoga and Social Justice." She'd spoken about collective suffering and said that to bridge the gap between white people and Black people and people of color in order to begin eradicating racism, we needed to tap into collective suffering together in order to understand how to truly move forward.

How do we do this? With breath.

Recently, I've noticed many women getting involved in this fight, white women in particular. Let's be clear - Black women have always been in the fight. But why were so many white women motivated to take part? Because they could relate to the exact moment when George called out for his mama. They felt that moment in their bodies, their breasts, and in their wombs. All women have an awareness of motherhood, whether they've birthed children or not. There is within us an understanding that goes back centuries, if not millenia. It is this that helps us tap into collective suffering. I watched as these white women fought for Black lives as if the Black boys dying were their own sons, using their voices to demand justice. Breath.

It comes back to trauma. Slavery traumatized Black people in a way that it remains in their DNA, their bloodlines. On the flip side, white supremacy has infected white people so deeply thanks to the programming and fearmongering that it's in their DNA, too, and because of that pervades the court systems, prisons and jails, the police, and even housing.

Police officers are traumatized almost daily in their work from all they see and the actions they're often forced to take to rectify a situation. They're angry, frightened, and constantly living on the knife edge of fight or flight, except they're trained to fight, not take flight. They don't have the option to pause since doing so could put a life in danger.

They've been taught either through words, actions, or experiences that Black men especially could be behind their trauma, which taints the kind of clear thinking that's desperately needed in extreme situations. It blurs the lens through which they see and experience the world.

When I was in rehab, I not only learned much about myself, but also about other people, white men in particular. They are suffering as well. I was able to find empathy for everyone in rehab because of the shared addiction fueled by trauma. In rehab I met criminals, police officers, priests, including some that abused young boys, and some of the boys that had been abused. I sat in prayer with construction workers, high-profile Wall Street-type rich white men, and homeless war veterans. Yes, there were women, but far fewer than there were men.

What was incredible to me was watching the men of all races

break down in tears as they talked about being sexually abused as boys and men, physically abused as children, and neglected beyond comprehension. Their stories were some of the saddest I'd ever heard, sadder even than mine. They then talked about the social difficulties of not being able to show emotion for fear of being seen as weak. Societal norms had them convinced that they needed to provide for their families, or they were worthless.

There were men in rehab who came out after living lives of painstaking secrecy, each one terrified to reveal their truth. There were Black transgender people who had felt different their entire lives, suffering extreme bullying and abuse for their differences. There were Black, indigenous, and other people of color (BIPOC) that had experienced ongoing racial trauma and had come to believe the problem was them, not the way society chose to treat them.

People often ask me how I'm able to sympathize with so many people, especially white, male Republicans that either appear racist or openly are. The answer is simple: those are the men that protected me during detox and rehab. Those are the ones that put me under their wing and cheered me on when I was falling apart. And I held their hands when their wives and children didn't show on visiting day because the reality of seeing their loved one in rehab one more time was too much. I sat with cops you might define as having conservative ideals while they cried about killing young people, white and Black, with so much fear and guilt regarding the meaning of life. If I saw those men today, I know they would be the first to help me no matter what I needed, no matter their supposed views.

Human connection is vital. When humans connect through their pain, suffering, struggle, and hope, it is incredibly powerful. We all want to feel okay in the world, even the folks you assume don't care. The truth is, addiction and trauma bonded us like nothing else could have. Those people, from the racist white guys to the Wall Street wannabes, became my best friends in rehab. Many still are to this day. We cried together, we did yoga together, we relived our worst nightmares together, and we breathed. Together.

Breath is like a little love note to our bodies, our souls. It brings air and love into the places we need it to in order for us to survive. It helps create the love we need for humanity, to help us keep on keepin' on until we finally have enough faith in ourselves and in our world. Breath holds space for our spirits when we doubt whether we can go on. It is the unconditional love that our parents never gave us, but that we gave ourselves. It is the gentle gift of tenderness our inner child might not have gotten on the outside, but fostered within. It was with me in detox and rehab, in every hospitalization, and in every moment I sobbed uncontrollably, begging for my pain to just please go away already.

Breath saved my life. It can save yours, too. It's always with you, the one constant we can count on until our time comes and we die. And even then, we are grateful because it gave us, our bodies and minds, what we needed when our souls were still in their earthly vessels. It only leaves us when we no longer need it.

So, when you're struggling to wrap your mind around yet another racist thing that came out of the mouth of yet another prominent public official, pause. Remember that racism is finally trying to find its way out of our system, globally and nationally. It just keeps bumping up against age-old fears that are slowly beginning to dissipate as we all just breathe.

"After all, in the end, we're all just humans trying to walk each other home." - Ram Dass

34

JOEY, COVID, ADDICTION AND INEQUALITY

I met Joey in rehab. We were in every group together. He was tough, had more than a lot on his proverbial plate, and had already spent time in jail. I didn't warm up to him right away, but as time went on it was obvious this guy had a heart of gold.

When you're in places like rehab, you get to know people very quickly and get to see almost immediately who they truly are behind the tears, anger, hurt, and utter vulnerability. He was as guarded as I was, but we came to trust each other. It's strange how in rehab you befriend people you might not have otherwise. I was lucky to call Joey my friend.

We had a lot of laughs in spite of our challenging circumstances. There were some really good days in rehab, and some really horrible days, days we would find things out about our families we didn't want to learn. Days full of the pain of missing loved ones on the outside. Days of not knowing what our future held and the fear that not knowing brought us each day. Fear that our demons were stronger than our hopes. Even days when we had push-up challenges that I sometimes won. (Okay, he might have let me.)

On the bad days he would write me notes, always with a smiley face in them. I was always so fearful of being a good mom to my daughter during this time and Joey was excellent at helping me feel seen and heard with no judgment. He met Blessing and reassured me often that I had nothing to worry about.

Although he was an incredible human being, he did get caught up in some stuff while in his active addiction that he had to face. He left rehab to go to court a week before I was discharged. We prayed together that day that maybe he wouldn't get locked up, even though we both knew he would. We discussed how, if that happened, he would stay sober, well enough, and hopeful. That was the last time I saw him.

In April of 2020, Joey died of an overdose. It was the early days of the COVID-19 pandemic in this country and across the world, so the untimely death of an addict didn't raise many eyebrows. COVID had grabbed the headlines everywhere and with a stronghold that, as of this writing, remains.

I might not have a full perspective on the pandemic, but I do have some opinions based on observations. The pandemic has killed thousands of people. More than a quarter of a million and that number is still rising. It has isolated us with its necessary mandates and lockdowns, destroyed economies across the planet, and has especially damaged small businesses. It didn't help that our president was far more concerned with feeding his ego during an election year than actually doing something to prevent people from dying.

And yet, liquor stores were considered an essential business. More people die annually from overdose and alcohol-related issues than almost any other cause, and that number has been climbing during the pandemic, and yet liquor stores are essential. What?!

Isolation is one of the primary triggers for relapsing, and somehow in the midst of an unthinkable pandemic, officials decided to make it easier for people to do far more than fall off the wagon. When the pandemic first hit Cape Cod's shores and forced everything around us to close, it also took away the life-lines of countless people in recovery: meetings, support groups, connecting with programs.

In early recovery, people often go through a process called 90 in 90, or 90 meetings in 90 days. Some people go to one a day, while others go to more than one, all in an attempt to feel "normal" again. We have created a culture of teaching people to become so dependent upon attending meetings that when they're not there, some addicts simply can't function. Thanks to COVID, we took away the life raft and left the ocean of alcohol, in which addicts everywhere were forced to sink or swim.

Because so many people weren't taught the coping skills necessary for getting through such challenging times, it's no wonder addiction and overdose rates started creeping up. There was no mindfulness for people to rely on, no awareness that it was possible to exist without meetings. Isolation is a real problem right now and if someone doesn't know how to manage difficult emotions, PTSD, or painful triggers on their own by using mantras, meditation, breathing, and mindfulness, relapses will be a regular occurrence.

It's possible that's what happened to Joey. I wrote to him every chance I could while he was in jail, encouraging him to remember that he was strong enough to get through it. He tried his best to stay positive, but no matter what trauma you've experienced before you go to prison, what you witness inside can be much worse.

But he did get out and we continued to write, even after he relapsed and went back to jail. When he got out again, I was hopeful that we'd connect again. He was one of the first people to believe in the dream I had of creating my business, B FREE.

I thought about Joey in contrast to COVID. Because there were so many people flooding hospitals, they needed to make more room in other places to treat people who didn't have COVID. I couldn't help but think about what it would be like if they did that with addiction and severe mental illness. What if people treated them as a health emergency the same way we've treated COVID?

In the beginning, many people with addiction were turned away from getting support because priority was given to patients with COVID-19. I understand, but let's be clear about the choices we make regarding human life. We deem certain people as more important than others and act accordingly. Just because we didn't hear about the numerous addiction deaths on the nightly news doesn't mean they didn't happen or have a similar impact on the families of those lost, just like COVID.

We also prioritize who we treat based on race. What about all of the Black folks and people of color in struggling neighborhoods, living in poverty and without the health insurance needed to seek help both for COVID and other illnesses? It's no surprise that COVID-19 hit communities of color far harder than any other. Our society survives on the backbones of people of color forced to work less than minimum wage jobs with no health insurance just to try and feed their families. I am in awe of such people, those who do their best to feel like worthy humans in this society we've created.

COVID not only robbed us of our ways of life, it also took away our connection to each other and redirected it to our phones, tablets, computer screens, and televisions. Suddenly, we had a nation of people addicted to social media and the constant breaking news headlines. Meanwhile, Big Media carefully culled images to ensure that the divide created by politics would widen further. It got so that no one knew the truth about who started what riot, or who was protesting peacefully. Black Lives Matter was labeled a terrorist organization, and armed white people pointed guns from their front lawns at protestors who were simply holding signs.

Even now, it continues. My best advice is to get off your screens and get on your mats. Sit. Sift through the information you know to be true from the perspective of a human being. Get back to being grounded and understand that, overall, the general nature of people is goodness. People often call me crazy when I say that. But we were all born as loving beings into this world. It is what we've been taught that has colored how we see things. The goodness gets lost as we learn to judge, to condemn, to hate, regardless of what race we are.

We can change that. As one of my favorite authors, Glennon Doyle, said in her book, *Untamed*, "We can do hard things." And we can. We can pause. We can think. We can stop, and we can breathe.

✻ 35 ✻

POUND IT OUT

Several things saved my life. My daughter, my husband, rehab, and yoga are at the top of the list. But POUND is keeping me alive. WTF is POUND? POUND is a fitness activity unlike any other and combines the use of weighted drumsticks with some intense and fun physical movement. Instead of listening to the music, you embody it and learn all the magnificent ways your body kicks ass.

Being a POUND Pro has taken my life full circle. Both times I was in rehab, I went to the same place, Recovering Champions. Both times I was welcomed with arms wide open. It was here that I discovered the powerful tools of yoga and breath, which inspired me to heal my addiction further by becoming a certified yoga teacher, and then a POUND Pro.

When I'd completed my second rehab stay, I returned home to be a wife, a mother, and to complete my yoga teacher training. Four months later, I'd earned my certificate, and a month after that, became a POUND Pro. No small feat, if I do say so. Though I was terrified and riddled with self-doubt, I breathed through each challenging moment, sometimes screaming out my frustrations as I banged that stick on the floor.

POUND, like yoga, is my church. It is the place where I get to beat the shit out of the floor, scream, sweat, bounce around to loud music, and let go of stuff like I never have before *and* enjoy doing it. I've found that POUND really speaks to those who don't feel they have a voice. It helps them connect to their inner power as they keep the beat in their hearts. And now I get to teach it.

I've taught it at my studio, and at the rehab facility that welcomed me twice. I will never forget the first time I saw the smiles light up the faces of those in recovery during a POUND class. I wanted to bottle it up for them, knowing that such joy can be so fleeting during treatment. I'll also not forget the moment I heard them take a deep, collective breath between the walls that I stared at for 60 some-odd days, not knowing how I was going to survive in the outside world.

POUND reminds me that things *can* change. That life can change. That YOU can change. It's about finding what you need in order to be your best self, able to live your truth fiercely, proudly, out loud, one beat at a time.

❧ 36 ❧

WISDOM, JUSTICE, LOVE, AND FREEDOM

"Radical simply means grasping things at the root" - Angela Davis

I f you're reading this book and don't know who Angela Davis is, get to knowing. She is one of the most amazing badass Black women advocates there is. She is one of the brave souls in this world that advocated for herself and the rights of others in relation to the social justice system. I think often of her words, especially when I'm thinking about racial injustice and the U.S. Prison System.

It is my firm opinion, one that is shared by countless others, that it's no accident that Black men are the majority of those incarcerated. I'm not saying every single one is innocent, but I am saying it's a social construct. Let me explain further.

Prisons have a function in society and that is to house those who have committed crimes. But a closer look at those imprisoned reveals there is more to it than merely committing a crime.

Far too many people in jail are there due to poverty, trauma, addiction, and lack of access to mental health services. At the forefront of this disparity is racism, particularly against Black men. Black men represent what America is really afraid of: them having power.

Our system is so broken that it continues to operate under one guiding force: fear. Think back to each of the people and their stories that I met and heard while in rehab. Those are the humans that fill our prisons, where there is no rehabilitation, no addiction treatment, no promise of any kind of healing. You are labeled and those labels are nearly impossible to shake.

Sadly, many people in rehab have done time, save for those (primarily white men) that could afford top-notch lawyers that advocated for rehab instead of jail. While not every Black man is unable to afford a decent attorney, far too many are, which means that white men end up with better representation and services. We also need to remember that who ends up in prison also has quite a lot to do with who is deemed worthy in our society and to our social justice system, and far too often, if you're not white, you're not worthy.

But there is always, always hope. Hope lives in all of us, even if we can't feel its presence. Each of us deserves hope, and we also deserve to feel free. Each one of us. Freedom shouldn't be something dictated by our lineage, heritage, or ancestry, nor our ethnicity. We shouldn't become separated from it simply because our skin color differs from another's. Every single one of us - my mother, my niece, my daughter, my stepsons, my husband, and my brother - deserves to know freedom.

When freedom isn't given to us, or worse, is stripped away, it can feel debilitating. Folks who have endured significant trauma in their lives understand this best. They feel as though their lives have been stolen, that their stories are over before even being written.

I don't believe this is true. If I've learned anything in this life, it's that we get to create our own stories. We are not stuck in them simply because it might seem that way. None of us are. We get to decide, to choose what comes next. We can create our worth, choose our paths, just as the recovering alcoholic wakes up each day and chooses sobriety.

If you're upset by the injustices of the world, find a way to make change. Get up and get active in some kind of activism, be it anti-racism, empowerment of women, or equal rights for LGBTQ+ people. Get creative, figure out what actions you can take, and stand in your fucking power when you do.

Historian Laurel Thatcher Ulrich once said, "Well behaved women seldom make history." That is a true statement. think about it: the only reason women have the rights and freedoms of the 21st century (working, voting, holding office) *because* of the countless women that came before them and fought hard for those rights. Many of us have had to fight for our place in a male-dominated society. Ruth Bader Ginsberg did and understood well the importance of supporting women in enacting change. She created a path for women to be seen as real, intelligent, strong, and worthy in this society. I say we honor her wishes and embody what freedom looks like.

So what does it look like? Well, that answer will be different for everyone. For those dealing with domestic violence, it might look like finally getting free from your abuser. For veterans living with PTSD, it might look like getting a peaceful and complete night's sleep. For addicts, it might mean seeing a liquor store and no longer feeling that pull to step inside.

For the police, it might look like freedom to speak and live your truth as you open dialogue on issues you didn't previously feel safe discussing. For people of color, it might mean being brave enough to heal emotionally from too many traumas as you learn to thrive instead of just survive. For some white people, it might mean stepping up as an ally and persevering even after you've gotten it wrong five times before getting it right through a policy change that sparks reform. For certain women, it might look like getting a promotion or a key job based on your intellect and ability, and not the fact that you have tits and a vagina. For parents, it might look like taking some time to yourselves without guilt, knowing that you're taking care of your kids by taking care of yourself.

The list goes on and on depending upon who is making the choices. Freedom might simply look like waking up in the morning and doing your best to be yourself, whatever that means. It might be smiling during a difficult day when you think you can't. It might be hugging your kid at the end of the day, knowing there is nowhere else you'd rather be in that moment.

Freedom is staying present, using your breath, and remaining grounded, rooted, and radical in your own way. It could mean turning off your phone, your computer, the television, or your tablet and just being with the people you love, surrounded by human kindness.

For me, freedom is looking at my husband and loving him for all that he is, including the scars both visible and hidden. It is looking at my beautiful Blessing and knowing that she was named such because she is truly a Blessing to this family and to our world. It is looking at my stepsons and feeling more pride in being part of their lives than I thought possible.

I feel freedom when I move my body. When I dance. When I look at someone in the grocery store and smile, and they smile back, their eyes crinkling in that familiar way above their mask. I feel free when I talk about social justice issues and can see the moment someone makes a connection with my words by the expression on their face. I feel free when I hear my daughter let out a full belly laugh in the back of the car on the way home from school or on the way to the beach. I feel free on the beach with the sun beaming down, the wind ruffling my hair, and the waves crashing gently along the shore.

I feel free in writing this book and getting sloppy puppy kisses from my dog. I am so fucking lucky, and so very blessed to be in this life. We all are. Everything is happening *for* us, not to us. We are, as the saying goes, spiritual beings having a human experience. All is as it is supposed to be. Imagine that, and then, well, do something with it. Live *your* truth, appreciate your life, own your freedom.

37

CREATING FREEDOM THROUGH
BECOMING FREE

W hile in rehab for the second time, once again on my yoga mat, I was forever changed. This was the moment I figured out that I could actually change my own thinking by using my breath. It shifted the world for me in a way that made me feel as though I'd crossed the bridge from addiction to recovery simply by breathing. It felt glorious, and I felt, well, free.

I knew in that moment I wanted to teach people what I'd learned. I *had* to. Before I had a business model, I would tell anyone and everyone who would listen that there was a way out. There was a way to be in recovery *and* enjoy life. It came down to using your breath and moving your body.

It was different from 12-step groups like AA, NA, or any other A. Instead, I felt like I had the power to heal myself from the inside out instead of searching for a meeting, a phone number, or a big book that supposedly had all the answers, though none ever resonated with me quite like this. I was fucking FREE.

I started writing down every thought I had about movement, the body, the breath, and connecting them in order to recover from anything and everything. As time went on, a business model began to take shape. I realized that I had a healing method that could be used by anyone, regardless of what they were seeking healing for, be it addiction (food, drugs, sex, alcohol, shopping), or unhealed trauma.

Trauma is an especially big piece of the puzzle for me. In each of my rehab stays and in my work with others, I've never met a single person without some past trauma. Often, many of those living in the shadow of trauma are also in active addiction. Even the folks that don't drink or do any type of drug can still be addicts. They can have food addictions, sex addictions, even shopping addictions. Behind them all is unhealed trauma.

I've been challenged on this when leading groups for addiction recovery, especially by men. They're adamant that the trauma piece isn't true. They make excuses about how they partied too much in college and developed a habit. I'd tell them that if that was it, they wouldn't be stuck in a rehab center with a disease that affects the brain so powerfully that you have no control over it.

Trauma is anything the brain perceives as traumatic at any given moment. It could be an event that happened as early as in utero, at birth, or during the toddler years, or it could be something that happened later in life. It can be passed to us from our ancestors. It's in every Black body that has ethnicity that can be traced back to slavery. Because of ongoing racism, Black people are born on alert and remain that way throughout their lives, a tiring and draining existence.

Our bodies were created to protect us, and that includes the brain, which knows only how to fight, flee, or freeze. We learned these acts of protection as primitive beings running from dinosaurs, and our brains are still trying to catch up. Some of us that were blessed to have access to decent healthcare and mental health support are more aware of this and of the steps we can take to expand our minds. But for others mired in poverty, systemic racism, and internalized racism, the inherited traumas come with health problems, disease, and mental illness.

While we might not consciously remember the actual moment our brains made note of the trauma that we experienced, our bodies *always* remember. Always. "The issues are in our tissues," said Nikki Myers, creator of Yoga of 12 Step Recovery. The pain of trauma lives deep in our bodies, in our fibers, our tissues, our bones, our organs. If that trauma isn't resolved, we reach for something to calm the pain, be it physical or psychological. Sometimes it's too much food, and sometimes it's drugs or alcohol, or both. We think such measures work, and for a while they might, but it doesn't work out well in the end.

This is the exact reason I developed my B FREE coaching model. Through my own work, and my work with others, I designed a model on healing trauma in the body by giving that trauma what it needs in order to heal. It takes a combination of efforts. Simply sitting and talking without any type of movement or breath work isn't effective enough. Ask someone who's been in therapy for a long time. In some cases, the experience of rehashing their traumatic experiences only served to re-traumatize them.

My approach is different and starts with Freedom. The FREE in B FREE stands for Find. Recover. Evolve. Enjoy. We begin with finding ourselves. If we can't identify who we want to be, how can we find a way to get there? The Universe doesn't know how to guide you to what's meant for you without you having some awareness of who you want to be. This is your opportunity to create the self you've been longing for by getting clear and specific about how you see yourself using breath, visualization, and meditation.

Then we begin to recover. By identifying what we need to let go of, and becoming aware that it's safe to let it go, we begin to heal. More than that, as we move our bodies through yoga, dance, breath, and meditation, we let go of what we once were and make space for who we want to become. Writing down your discoveries is encouraged.

The big work comes with Evolve. At this stage we're getting into the nitty gritty of our shit. This is the time to dig deep, to find that place inside us where the pain lives and meet it head on. We might cry, scream, fuck some shit up, get angry, roar, and be as messy as we need to be to say goodbye to the parts that no longer serve us.

Then we practice, practice, practice using the tools we have learned - movement and mindfulness, writing and meditating - to begin creating exactly what we need. It's not as scary as it sounds, but it is work. It is the most poignant journey I've ever seen and experienced. I've had the privilege of witnessing profound change in people as I hold space for the growth they've been aching for finally finds them.

This is when we get to Enjoy. Here is where we flourish and celebrate all of the intense work we've done together. We learn about the power of the Universe and Spirit and the importance of maintaining the mind-body-spirit connections as we manifest our dreams. The key to realizing your dreams is simple: connection. The Universe is looking for a connection with you. Once that's been established, life becomes about trusting the path the Universe provides, and enjoying the ride.

I'm not saying bad shit won't still happen. But when you're armed with tools like mindfulness, breath work, movement, and a way to process your emotions, challenges, and even positives, the bad shit doesn't feel nearly as bad as it once did.

Everyone's path is different. What someone's coaching model looks like depends on what they're up against, what they're working with, and what they're willing to give in order to get where they want to be. I've worked with women living in situations of domestic violence. With veterans living with severe PTSD that prevents them from sleeping. People in recovery from substance abuse. People who simply feel alone. B FREE has helped each of them.

For the veterans, I encourage spending a good deal of time in restorative yoga poses and working with the breath. Sometimes breathing is all we do - in and out, slowly, mindfully. As I am also a Reiki practitioner, I will often infuse yoga with energy healing. The yoga, especially, helps give the mind and body space to just be. The body is supported through the pose, making it feel safer to breathe in a particular way. The body is able to heal since it has been allowed to slow down and return to the state it was before we grew overwhelmed.

Sometimes, though, even when we breathe our primitive minds can still take us to our most frightening moments. That's when being with someone who is aware of this becomes extremely important. I've been in emotional places with people where all you can do is hold their hand as they push through the pain to find the light. I've comforted veterans and survivors of violence as they cried in restorative poses. I've held space while they spoke aloud things they'd been needing to say, but didn't feel safe enough before. Sometimes, just witnessing someone's pain without fear or judgment is enough for them to feel safe, to keep going, to keep healing.

Slowly, I began networking my new business. When someone asked me what I did for a living, I eagerly told them that I was the owner and founder of B FREE Coaching and Wellness. It rolled out of my mouth like I'd been doing it for years. With each interaction, I'd get more focused about the program, aware of the minute details that were important to its success. It felt as though it poured out of me, in spite of the fact that I was making it through each networking event on nothing but the power of seltzer water and a slice of lime.

As the business model came together, I asked a friend if she was still renting office space in a building I'd seen a few months prior. I visited the location and was thrilled to find that it would work, then called Jason on the spot and told him to meet me there and bring the checkbook. He sighed, no doubt concerned, but came. We left with the keys to B FREE in hand.

The next day brought a trip to Ikea where I picked out furniture for the new office. The entire time I was musing about what came first, the chicken or the egg. Did I get the office first or was B FREE already so well-formed that it led to the office being secured? What was the future of this thing I'd created? All I knew was that coursing through my body was this incredible feeling of *yes*. Everything was working as it was meant to.

As time went on, and my classes in Pound, yoga, and Zumba grew in popularity, I realized I needed a different, larger space. For a while, I shared a studio space with another studio owner, but realized I genuinely needed something of my own. While lying on the floor in savasana, I thought about how I just needed to create that space. Ironically, or not, while my husband and I were away on a weeklong yoga retreat in Cuba, something went awry with the space I was in and I could no longer use it. I opened my own, official B FREE studio in June of 2019, a simple but fabulous place where people can come to breathe, move, and just be.

I see my success in unique ways, often in the form of phone

calls from the partners of people I've worked with, thanking me for helping. Their husbands are less angry, are able to look them in the eye again, are more patient, and are able to sleep at night. Some have lessened their drinking, or quit it altogether, and others took steps toward recovery.

Now, B FREE is about to gain non-profit status in order to help us to better serve those that need it most. The first coaching training starts this February (2021) in which 10 new coaches will be born in June ready to save the world. My vision for my business is to create a full wellness center that incorporates various modalities in helping heal humans and all of their wonderful parts.

Healing isn't just about the physical self, and we don't just get sick physically. We often get sick as a result of stress on the mind and the body. In order to heal humans as whole beings, we need to treat them in mind, body, and spirit. That's why the long-term goal for B FREE is to create a center that includes medical practitioners, pediatricians, psychologists, therapists, psychiatrists, herbalists, massage therapists, reiki practitioners, and healers of all kinds, ideally working under one roof to provide real healing for everyone.

There will be a strong focus on people in recovery, and I believe the model B FREE uses will become something other organizations can adopt. I know from experience that Cape Cod desperately needs such a place, given its soaring rates of addiction, and other parts of the country do, as well.

Race is also an important factor. Far too often, the majority of people in a yoga studio are white. But everyone needs healing. We're all recovering from something, no matter our skin color. I aim to make B FREE a safe space for everyone of any shade of the rainbow and have already begun enacting change through Love and Revolution, a group I started on Facebook in honor of

George Floyd and Ahmaud Arbery. It became clear to me that their deaths had an impact even on this mostly white peninsula, and that Cape Codders *do* care. They just needed to gain a little knowledge.

Love and Revolution is a place where resources toward ending racism can be found and shared, and eradicating racism is the goal. We have an understanding that everyone is on their own journey of unlearning racism, and the group is a fantastic place for people to connect. I'm proud that the group has become such a force of nature, and of the work that has already been done. As B FREE evolves, I'm looking forward to adding a library and meeting space dedicated to anti-racist education, to be dubbed "The Room of Love and Revolution." I'm excited to see the growth that emerges.

38

TIME TO SHINE

T his note goes out to moms everywhere, but particularly those in recovery, be they at the beginning of their healing journey or whether they've been sober for years. But let me be clear - we're all recovering from something, whether we've expressed it through addiction or not.

Parenting is really hard. I mean *really* hard. Fraught with tension and worry and insecurity and doubt and elation and frustration and just about every other emotion you can think of. It is, without a doubt, the most difficult thing I've ever done, and still is.

When you're a mother trying to recover from trauma and you don't have all of your tools yet, and are still reaching for another sip, another glass, another bottle of wine to cope, parenting is especially challenging. Our children, even without knowing it, can retraumatize us, reverting us internally right back to the age we were when our original trauma took place.

I have worked with women who are survivors of sexual abuse. Sometimes, they feel they're okay. Then their child turns the age they were when the abuse occurred, or the age they became aware of the abuse, it becomes too much for their brains and hearts to bear. They find themselves in the hospital in need of mental health care, or, like me, rehab.

It happens, and it's okay.

Let me say that again - It happens *and* it's okay.

I'm here to tell you to remove all judgment of yourself as a parent, a mother, a wife, or whatever other role you're convinced you need to be perfect at. There is no such thing. Not one person has it completely right. Also, what other people think of you is none of your fucking business. It's time to stop trying to impress them, to impress the world, with your "skills."

This is perhaps the greatest life lesson I've learned so far. I said it many times at the first retreat I held through my personal wellness company, Becoming FREE, and it really resonated with people. I truly hope it does the same with you. The truth is that the only person who defines you is you. The important question isn't "how do I want to look?" but "how do I want to feel?" Design your life according to how you want to feel and how you'd like others to feel after spending time with you.

Now, back to the parenting piece. I'm going to be brutally honest here: I don't like being a mom. I love my kid more than anything else in this world. She is, without a doubt, the best thing that ever happened to me. But I don't like the role of being a mother. It is draining to be needed that much. It's overwhelming to take genuine care of myself and be in recovery while also taking care of my daughter.

Parenting is different for everyone, and, unless you're intentionally harming your child in some way, none of it is bad or wrong. It's just different. We create our parenting model based on what we believe, and to some degree, by either emulating or soundly rejecting what we lived as children. Jason loves being a dad. He loves being needed by his daughter and by me, by his sons, and even by the people at his job. This seemed to be a problem between us until I started defining my role as a mom and wife in a way that worked for me and my kid. It is definitely still evolving, and always will. What helps is acknowledging what I need, which is a lot of space.

I need to be able to get away sometimes without feeling guilty. Just to be me and do what brings me joy: write, breathe, yoga, to hear my own thoughts and spend time being grateful for this beautiful life I get to have.

I have friends that ask me all the time how I'm able to live my life as I do. I tell them that for me, it's just not worth it to live a life you don't want to be fully part of all the time. What's the point of that? Of staying somewhere you're not happy or with someone you're not happy with? Ask yourself what keeps you in a place of unhappiness, aside from your children, your house, or your job.

The excuses can go on and on, but it's important to recognize them as excuses. That's how you get to the real answer. If it's fear, then what is it a fear of? Define it and I can assure you that once you name the fear, it will feel much less threatening, especially since fear isn't real anyway. We create fear in the moment, believing that we need it in order to maintain control. Newsflash: no one is really in control, either. Not even that perfect yoga mom with the organic cotton leggings, recycled mat, and matching mani-pedi.

Sit with that a while. Meditate on it. Take a walk with it and let it bounce around a bit. Let the answers come without judging yourself. Let them become crystal clear, so much so there's only surety. We all know what's real and true in our bodies, especially moms. We're simply afraid we might need to make some changes in how we take care of ourselves that might look different from what we've been told parenting "should" look like.

When I was in rehab, I kept thinking, "Every mom needs to do this!" Every mother deserves 28 days to focus only on herself, on her own mental health and well-being. We had our meals cooked using foods from the on-site garden, were driven to places we needed, had our meds delivered to us, and went to sleep at a reasonable hour. We were cared for inside and out.

When I have taken care of myself and gotten away for a little while, even if just one day, I am so much more capable of loving my daughter. Because I'm not fighting against my own needs, or feeling deprived, I can be fully present with her, which is what she deserves.

A friend asked me a while back what she should do about her marriage, which had proven unfulfilling. She'd been married to the same man since she was in her teens and wasn't sure she wanted to be any longer. She described someone else she'd met and how wonderful she felt with him, how rejuvenated and revived. I kept telling her that her decisions depended upon how she defined marriage. That it depended upon how she wanted to define love in her life at that moment, how a love that brought her happiness would look and feel. That it depended upon how she saw herself in her future - was it in a meaningful, true way, or something that might leave her feeling empty again?

She giggled and told me she liked the way I thought. I took it further and removed the labels "good" and "bad" and "right" and "wrong" from the equation. We've been taught that ending a marriage is "bad" unless someone is in physical danger. We've been taught that sticking it out through the lonely times is "good." Is it? Really? In truth, it all comes down to how you define it. "It all depends on how you define 'wrong,'" I told my friend with a smile. (Sometimes I wonder if this is what keeps my dad and Maggie together.)

We can design our lives the way we want. As cliché as it sounds, it's true. It's up to us to draw the plans, create the map, and make it happen. But somewhere along the way, we get blocked by concerns that we're not doing things the way we "should" be. The first thing I tell people in coaching is to remove the word "should" from their vocabulary. Life, emotions, and even love are not linear. They are fluid and moveable and flow like rivers. There is no straight and narrow anything, and everything brings with it a lesson.

Addicts getting into recovery know this best. If I blamed myself or gave in to all the guilt and shame I felt when I relapsed after six months sober, I would still be drinking. Actually, I'd likely be dead. Shame and guilt have no place in our lives to the level we've elevated them. Yes, we should feel bad for hurting someone, but to carry years of shame and guilt around with us like massive boat anchors is an exercise in futility. All it does is get you stuck firmly in a place you desperately want to get out of, but can no longer figure out how.

Instead of getting stuck in that place of what I "should" have done, I celebrated the fact that I was alive. If I was alive, I could still grow and change and be. I could raise a fist instead of a glass. I could raise a sign. I could raise my vibration. That's what made me dance and do yoga in detox. The awareness that I was *still here*. My relapse didn't kill me. Because of that, I was more alive than I'd ever felt before and was able to open my eyes to new ways of being, of thinking that I'd not seen before. I rejoiced in making the choice to continue to remain sober, now aware of what going on a major bender would have done instead.

It is important to value yourself enough to welcome change. To allow it and roll with it and let it take you to new places. See yourself as someone of value, of someone the world is better of having in it. How we choose to view ourselves is what lights the way toward real healing.

It is time for you to shine and find out what it means to be free.

ACKNOWLEDGMENTS

To those fighting addiction, you have everything you need and already are a miracle. All the staff at Recovering Champions that helped to save my life. All the staff and board members of B FREE that help keep the dream alive. To Maggie & my dad for trying to parent through their trauma, and being there when my mom couldn't. My editor, my friend, Kat Szmit for walking in my shoes with me. Wicked Whale Publishing and Graphics for bringing these words into the world.

ABOUT THE AUTHOR

Ayanna and her Mother

Ayanna Niambi Parrent lives on Cape Cod with her daughter Blessing, husband Jason, and their dog Sawyer. Her oldest stepson Holden attends UMass Amherst and her youngest stepson Sean is a senior at Sturgis Charter Public School with plans to join the Army after his 2021 graduation. Ayanna is the executive director, owner, and founder of B FREE Coaching and Wellness, Inc., located in Harwich Port, Massachusetts. For more information, visit bfreewell.com or email the author at befreewellinfo@gmail.com. Donations to the B FREE Non-Profit can also be made through the donation page on the website.